T0319457

Agile by
Design

Wiley & SAS Business Series

The Wiley & SAS Business Series presents books that help senior-level managers with their critical management decisions.

Titles in the Wiley & SAS Business Series include:

Demand-Driven Inventory Optimization and Replenishment: Creating a More Efficient Supply Chain by Robert A. Davis

Developing Human Capital: Using Analytics to Plan and Optimize Your Learning and Development Investments by Gene Pease, Barbara Beresford, and Lew Walker

The Executive's Guide to Enterprise Social Media Strategy: How Social Networks Are Radically Transforming Your Business by David Thomas and Mike Barlow

Economic and Business Forecasting: Analyzing and Interpreting Econometric Results by John Silvia, Azhar Iqbal, Kaylyn Swankoski, Sarah Watt, and Sam Bullard

Financial Institution Advantage & The Optimization of Information Processing by Sean C. Keenan

Foreign Currency Financial Reporting from Euros to Yen to Yuan: A Guide to Fundamental Concepts and Practical Applications by Robert Rowan

Harness Oil and Gas Big Data with Analytics: Optimize Exploration and Production with Data Driven Models by Keith Holdaway

Health Analytics: Gaining the Insights to Transform Health Care by Jason Burke

Heuristics in Analytics: A Practical Perspective of What Influences Our Analytical World by Carlos Andre Reis Pinheiro and Fiona McNeill

Human Capital Analytics: How to Harness the Potential of Your Organization's Greatest Asset by Gene Pease, Boyce Byerly, and Jac Fitz-enz

Implement, Improve and Expand Your Statewide Longitudinal Data System: Creating a Culture of Data in Education by Jamie McQuiggan and Armistead Sapp

Killer Analytics: Top 20 Metrics Missing from your Balance Sheet by Mark Brown

Predictive Analytics for Human Resources by Jac Fitz-enz and John Mattox II

Predictive Business Analytics: Forward-Looking Capabilities to Improve Business Performance by Lawrence Maisel and Gary Cokins

Retail Analytics: The Secret Weapon by Emmett Cox

Social Network Analysis in Telecommunications by Carlos Andre Reis Pinheiro

Statistical Thinking: Improving Business Performance, second edition by Roger W. Hoerl and Ronald D. Snee

Taming the Big Data Tidal Wave: Finding Opportunities in Huge Data Streams with Advanced Analytics by Bill Franks

Too Big to Ignore: The Business Case for Big Data by Phil Simon

The Value of Business Analytics: Identifying the Path to Profitability by Evan Stubbs

The Visual Organization: Data Visualization, Big Data, and the Quest for Better Decisions by Phil Simon

Understanding the Predictive Analytics Lifecycle by Al Cordoba

Unleashing Your Inner Leader: An Executive Coach Tells All by Vickie Bevenour

Using Big Data Analytics: Turning Big Data into Big Money by Jared Dean

Win with Advanced Business Analytics: Creating Business Value from Your Data by Jean Paul Isson and Jesse Harriott

For more information on any of the above titles, please visit www.wiley.com.

Agile by Design

An Implementation Guide to Analytic Lifecycle Management

Rachel Alt-Simmons

WILEY

Library of Congress Cataloging-in-Publication Data
Alt-Simmons, Rachel, 1971–
   Agile by design : an implementation guide to analytic lifecycle management / by Rachel Alt-Simmons.
        pages cm. – (Wiley & SAS business series)
   Includes bibliographical references and index.
   ISBN 978-1-118-90566-1 (cloth), ISBN 978-1-119-17715-9 (ePDF), ISBN 978-1-119-17716-6 (epub)
1. Business planning. 2. Organizational change. 3. Organizational effectiveness. 4. Management. I. Title.
   HD30.28.A3872 2016
   658.4'012–dc23
                                                                                  2015022015

Cover Design: Wiley
Cover Image: © iStock.com / Studio-Pro

10 9 8 7 6 5 4 3 2 1

Contents

Introduction

We live in a data-driven world. The analysis and business use of information is no longer a nice-to-have, but has increasingly become integral to our customer-critical business processes. Not only has data become a differentiator among businesses in terms of profitability but also in viability and longevity. While many organizations have relied on analysis and analytics for years, if not decades, the integration of insight into operational environments has not kept pace.

For some time, we've seen analytics move out of the basement and into the boardroom, as executives increasingly understand and embrace the role that information plays in their business. However, the execution (or operationalization) of that insight has not fully taken hold in the domain of IT. Part of the problem is that analytics groups have largely operated under the radar—their need for business agility and flexibility results in shadow IT organizations. Many analytic teams create and manage their own infrastructure. While this approach may offer some level of agility and flexibility, it doesn't create a sustainable path for growth or scale. In fact, many analytics groups become the victim of their own successes—creating mission critical predictive models or insight that cannot be easily ingested by the organization. Since they've been left out of the process for so long, IT teams tasked with supporting these new analytic projects struggle to keep up with what's needed for the projects; how to implement them; and, ultimately, how to support them longer-term. Business stakeholders are left unsure how to educate their staff or their customers in how analytics change the way they run their businesses.

Increasingly, organizations are finding that they can no longer operate in analytic silos. Business, analytic, and IT groups once at odds find that they are dependent on each other. Beyond addressing the technical and operational aspects, organizations need to address the organizational and cultural rifts that have built up over time—bringing the business, analytic groups, and IT organizations more closely in line.

Frustration and disappointment awaits the analysts who think their algorithms solve all business issues or replace people. While the modelers know how to dig into the data, the business customers know their business and potential implications. If they work collaboratively, the end result can provide a business with a competitive edge or at least stay abreast of the competition. In our years working with and on analytic teams, we know that adding the right amount of structure and rigor to an analytic project will help increase your chances of analytic success! Whether you're analytic pros or "new-bees," we think you'll find some opportunities to improve how you work together across the organization. Agile delivery techniques provide teams with a structured way to coordinate, communicate, and collaborate while embracing creativity and innovation.

The goal of this book is to assist organizations with the journey of integrating analytics with operational people and process infrastructure, allowing analytic teams to focus their time on innovative value-added projects. This allows the teams to wrap their work in the operational discipline essential to embedding analytics within the organization. Our approach is to extend agile delivery methods as a framework for execution, as it allows us to acknowledge the ambiguity inherent in analytic projects.

WHO SHOULD READ THIS BOOK

There's a little something for everyone inside this book:

Analytic teams

At its heart, this book is for you. *Agile by Design* provides a simple and flexible approach by taking the Scrum methodology as an effective way to execute and deliver on large analytic projects. Tools and techniques are offered to help the team showcase the value of their work within the organization; stay organized; and create a sustainable foundation for analytic delivery. At the same time, we want to help you better work with and understand the needs of your business and IT partners.

IT

For those of you who work with analytic teams, this book does not cover any deep technical approaches to analytics—that's a whole different book! But we do want to show you some ways that technologists and analysts can partner throughout a project and improve project time-to-value.

Business

Okay, business folks, you're not off the hook. After all, these analytic projects are for you; but maybe all that math is a little intimidating? Don't worry, there's no math in this book either: The intent is to help project teams come up with a common language and an engagement model for working together through the analytic project's duration.

Project Managers

Perhaps you're a project manager or ScrumMaster who's been handed the responsibility of managing one of these analytic projects, but the analytic team is resistant to being "managed." There are lightweight tools and examples that you can use with your teams to encourage engagement and keep the teams on track.

WHAT'S INSIDE

Read it all the way through, or find a chapter that's interesting to you. Remember, the beauty of agility is that you make it your own. If your team is having a problem with planning or prioritization, start there. If you need some help capturing some user stories, then go right to that chapter.

The book starts with an introduction to some of the changing market dynamics—your customers—that are making analytics more important to organizations across every industry. We reintroduce the topic of analytics to provide a definition for the types of insight and analysis people are generating. The analytic lifecycle is introduced within a business value chain framework, illustrating the importance of analytics in the broader context of implementation.

With the stage set, we kick it off with a hypothetical analytic project that we'll follow through to the end of the book. Customer-thinking concepts are introduced along with techniques for visioning your project and setting some concrete goals. The team then prioritizes their project against other important work going on at the company by performing some knowledge acquisition. With preliminary approval to begin some scoping work to see how big the project is, the team begins knowledge gathering activities. Working with their business and IT partners, the analysts will define their target variable and perform some initial data profiling and visualization activities to get an idea of the quality of their data.

Traditional and agile project delivery methods as well as an overview of the Agile Manifesto are provided. Using the manifesto as our guideline, we outline a delivery framework for analytics that leverages elements from two popular agile methodologies, Scrum and XP. As our project receives the green light from our executives, we start a formal planning cycle and define some common analytic work activities.

Next, the team uses a story-based approach to gather hypotheses from the business on what they believe to be the root cause of the analytic problem. By capturing hypotheses, the analytic team can start to prove or disprove some of the intuition-based reasoning with data-driven results. In order to gather an initial set of hypotheses, the team facilitates a story workshop to capture as many ideas as they can from the business.

An overview of the Scrum framework our team will be using is provided: This includes the day-to-day rhythm of the project. Roles and responsibilities are defined on the Scrum team, including the role of the business sponsor and product owner, and the responsibility of IT during the engagement. Our team kicks off the first planning cycle for their sprint and starts working. We follow the team through planning, execution, review, and retrospective.

Additionally, we turn to some of the analytic team's quality practices, bringing in several key engineering practices from the

XP methodology that will improve the overall quality of work and delivery. Collaboration and communication is also a focus area, where we provide some ideas for visualizing and communication day-to-day progress with the extended stakeholder group.

Once our model is complete, we prepare for a release. But while the model may be finished, the real work is just beginning. We'll initiate a business implementation planning session to determine how that model will be used by the business. This includes ideas for test-and-learn strategies and starting to create a culture of experimentation.

Finally, we'll deploy our model into the real world. We'll cover some of the different ways that organizations deploy models, how data is scored, and how those scores are used in other business applications.

THE COMPANION WEBSITE

Rome wasn't built in a day, and as such, this book will provide readers with a solid foundation of agile frameworks for analytics and how to use them to manage analytic projects, but there are always more details we don't have room to include! Additional goodies and other deep thoughts about agile analytic methodologies are available the companion website for this book, analyticscrum.com. On the site, you can download additional content and templates, read articles and posts, contribute, and ask questions.

About the Author

Rachel Alt-Simmons is an analytics and technology professional with 20 years of experience developing and integrating business analytic and technology strategies. Having worked across North and South America, she's helped Fortune 500 organizations build and continuously improve their analytic competencies.

She started her career in the mutual fund industry and moved into business intelligence and analytics leadership roles at The Hartford, where she built out an analytic competency center within the Global Wealth Management division.

Following that, she spent two years as research director for the Life and Annuity practice at the industry analyst firm TowerGroup before returning to the insurance industry. Rachel joined Travelers Insurance as part of a strategic leadership team to transform business intelligence and analytic capabilities within the Small Commercial division, and went on to create an enterprise analytic center of excellence.

In her role at SAS, Rachel works with customers across industry verticals to create customer-centric analytic processes, driving alignment between business and technology strategies.

In addition to her work at SAS, Rachel is an adjunct professor and agile coach at Boston University in the Computer Sciences department, teaching Agile Software Development, IT Strategy, and IT Project Management. Rachel is a Certified Lean Master, Six Sigma Black Belt, PMI Agile Certified Practitioner, and Project Management Professional.

A frequent industry speaker, writer, contributor, and thought leader, Rachel currently consults with companies across Canada, the United States, and Latin America on the strategic use of analytics and defining integrated approaches to aligning business and technology strategies.

CHAPTER 1

Adjusting to a Customer-Centric Landscape

Emerging customer needs and demands are driving a new imperative to align business, technology, and analytic strategies. With consumer forces forcing both rapid and dramatic change throughout every industry, companies need to take an outside-in approach to enable customer-centricity. A customer-centric organization aligns their business model to the customer's point of view, integrating functional areas, product lines, and channels to create 360° customer-centric business processes. Analytics facilitate the decision-making within those processes. Most companies lack the organizational structure to innovate quickly and are challenged by the scale of this transformational change. Agile approaches can be used to incrementally (ergo, more quickly) drive the transformation and create a fail-fast/succeed-sooner culture.

IT'S A WHOLE NEW WORLD

Just a few short years ago, if you wanted to buy something, you likely got into your car and drove to a store. Maybe the product you wanted was special and only one store in town offered the item. You arrived at the store and paid whatever price the store was asking because you really, really wanted it. Fast forward to today—instead of going to the store, you pick up your mobile device, tap a few buttons, and you find that same item available from dozens of online marketplaces. You select the cheapest price, and a drone drops it off on your doorstep the same day. You've also sold your car, since you don't need to drive to the store as much. It's much simpler to rent from a car-share service or be picked up by a ride-share service when you need it! This is a simple but common example of what tens of millions of people do every day.

The traditional businesses in this example—the physical stores, product manufacturers and distributors, and automakers—have all gone through tremendous change. Suppliers like Amazon.com changed the retail market by offering products quickly, increasing competition from suppliers from all over the world and putting pressure on them to offer those products at low prices. The landscape of online shopping has changed so much that you don't necessarily have to gravitate to the Amazons of the world anymore. Aggregation services have become pivotal in finding a particular item at the lowest price to be delivered in the quickest time (with minimal or free shipping & handling). Products can be sent directly from the manufacturer, obviating the need for the distributor. Car and ride-sharing services—part of our new "peer-to-peer" economy—are transforming (and disintermediating) the auto manufacturer and taxi industry.

This is great news for consumers: Globalization opens up new markets for companies while technology makes it easier to connect customers directly with products and services. But when traditional barriers to market entry are reduced or the market changes entirely, good and services become commodified and power shifts to the hands of the buyer. As consumers, the determination of how and when we get our goods and services has changed dramatically: We get to decide! Social media give us a voice, providing us with the opportunity to publicly promote or criticize a brand.

There are very few industries that have not been impacted by this change. Companies are struggling for relevance in an increasingly crowded and democratized marketplace. Here's why:

1. Technology connects consumers with products and services previously out of reach.

2. With ubiquitous access to products, services, and content in real-time, consumer expectations are heightened, and consumers are more educated and empowered.

3. As the cost of switching providers decreases, customers become less loyal.

4. With barriers to market entry reduced, new entrants flood the market, disrupting traditional business models.

5. Increased availability and accessibility commodifies products and services.

6. Distribution and communication channels rapidly evolve.

7. Product development cycles become shorter, decreasing first-to-market competitive advantage.

With so much access and buyer empowerment, many companies are unable to keep up with the pace of change. Many react by trying to compete on price. Yet differentiation isn't necessarily about the cost of goods. Organizations recognize that creating a positive and proactive customer experience across the customer lifecycle (from awareness to purchase to loyalty to advocacy) is critical to attracting and retaining profitable customers. In fact, as customers, we expect you to do it!

FROM CUSTOMER-AWARE TO CUSTOMER-CENTRIC

With the explosion of digital media, people engage with each other—and the companies they do business with—in new ways. The relevance of traditional print and broadcast channels are on the decline, completely changing the consumer-corporation dynamic. Digital channels open doors for consumers, who no longer are passive participants in a one-sided marketing conversation, but empowered authors, publishers, and critics. The digital landscape is participatory, an area where consumers exchange ideas. Marketers no longer drive the discussion. Everyday people are the style makers and trendsetters.

For companies competing in this new medium, it's incredibly difficult to surface your message above the noise. While the amount of time consumers spend on web and mobile has increased dramatically, the amount of available content has increased exponentially: More digital content is created in a day than most people can consume in a year. With so many distractions and choices, your audience has a very short attention span.

The exponential growth in digital channels has given rise to the importance of digital marketing. But digital marketing isn't just about the channel; it's the mechanism by which people are creating and sharing experiences: engaging not only with each other, but with companies they do business with.

For your financial services customers, there is no longer a traditional "path-to-purchase." The customer journey is no longer linear, and purchasing decisions are taking place across multiple channels: both physical and virtual. With such high channel fragmentation, making strategic decisions on audience, content, and platforms is critical. Companies need the capability to leverage data to define their market, build outstanding content, tailor messaging, and provide that messaging in the right medium—quickly!

With customer interactions constantly changing through your brand relationship, consumer behavior is difficult to predict. New consumer-driven tactics are emerging every week, making multi-month planning cycles a thing of the past: Your customer-centric strategy has to be adaptive and relevant. Slow and predictable internal processes must be replaced with quick and creative execution. You need to create a messaging that speaks to each audience segment differently. Data-driven approaches give you the ability to create that level of precision. Agility can speed up time-to-market cycles.

The entry point for becoming customer-centric is different for every organization. Many customer-centric strategies start with operational transformations, with the contact center as the new customer-centric hub. Around the hub, disjointed marketing campaign and contact strategies, customer relationship management strategies, product development, pricing and risk strategies, analytics, and operational strategies begin to synchronize—at least conceptually! For the first time, many companies are starting to view their operations from the outside in by mapping out the customer lifecycle and looking at ways to optimize that lifecycle across the organization.

There's a lot of complexity there. Executing on a large-scale transformation like this requires significant change. Organizationally, it necessitates a shift away from product silos to customer segments. Customer contact planning and execution strategies need to be coordinated and streamlined. The underlying operational technology platforms and systems need to connect in way to accommodate the customer-centric perspective. Cross-functional operational workflows need to be redesigned around a consumer view. The customer data needs to be integrated, analyzed, and modeled in a way to provide a comprehensive view of that customer. Analytics and predictive modeling provide insights to help anticipate customer needs and behavior. The entire organization mobilizes around the analytic customer-centric hub.

Our hub encompasses five core areas, as shown in Figure 1.1.

Business strategy The business strategy defines the types of projects that are important to the organization based on the needs of the market, customers, and the business. Analytic work must link back to strategic business goals.

Organization Organization defines the structure of the company, including the composition of teams and how they engage.

Figure 1.1 The Customer-Centric Analytic Hub Linked to Business Strategy

People The people category relates to individual roles, responsibilities, and skillsets needed to support the analytic hub.

Process Process defines the day-to-day interactions of internal and external parties throughout the organization. While this can include how teams engage in order to achieve a business objective, it also encompasses how your employees and operational systems interact with customers and suppliers.

Technology Technology provides the underlying platform to support the hub. Technology also includes the data needed to perform analysis.

BEING CUSTOMER-CENTRIC, OPERATIONALLY EFFICIENT, AND ANALYTICALLY AWARE

In our customer-centric world, business strategies are more enterprise in focus, requiring the integration and automation of business processes crossing functional, product, and channel boundaries. As organizations evolve out of their traditional product or functional silos to respond to the need for customer-centricity, their operating models must evolve with them.

As your customers' digital footprints grow through increased use of always-on mobile devices and social media as well as the transactional breadcrumbs they leave behind, they're expecting that that data will be used to their benefit.

> *Australian bank Westpac uses data-driven marketing and analytics in support of their "Know Me" program for their nine million customers. Westpac takes their customers' digital and transactional data and creates a picture of who that customer is, where they are in their life journey, and anticipate what needs they might have. Although their program is driven by the marketing organization, the bank is careful to take a service-oriented approach to their interactions. The benefits of the program have included higher conversion rates for offers and an increase in the number of products by household.[1]*

---

[1] Nadia Cameron, "Customer-Led Big Data Programs Deliver Millions to Westpac Bottom Line," CMO (February 24, 2014).

Data and technology enablers are changing the competitive landscape and providing capabilities for new product development and market penetration:

> *In late 2014, investment advisory firm Charles Schwab launched an automated online investment service called Robo Advisor. The system uses an algorithmic approach to automate portfolio management services. This low-cost service was created as way to reach an untapped market of investors, to "appeal to the masses and get more people into well-diversified portfolios."* [2]

These are just two examples in a sea of analytic innovation that's sweeping across industries. The operating model needed to support these types of initiatives bonds core business processes to technology infrastructure. The implementation strategies in our examples require the integration of several strategic areas within the organization, outlined in Figure 1.2, including business process automation, technology, analytics, and data.

Channel and Contact Strategy This is a critical (and sometimes neglected!) component of the overall hub. The contact strategy outlines how you will interact with customers, what their preferences are, and the optimal sequence of events. The contract strategy takes into account things like customer needs and

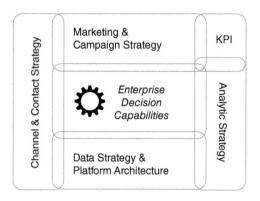

Figure 1.2 Enterprise Decision Capabilities

---

[2]Tara Siegel Bernard, "Schwab's Service for Investors Seeking Thrifty Advice Raises Eyebrows," *New York Times* (March 5, 2015).

preferences, offer-eligibility criteria, and campaign response history to ensure that the right offer is presented to the right customer in their preferred channel.

Marketing and Campaign Strategy Marketing teams provide the heartbeat of the process by coordinating the design and execution of the marketing strategy. This includes customer segmentation and analysis (**who** is my customer?), campaign planning (**what** are our organizational goals?), campaign operating rhythm (**how** do I get that message to my customer?), and campaign performance management (how **successful** are our campaigns?). Sophisticated organizations use optimization techniques in their planning process to balance the trade-offs between eligible campaign populations and available offers.

Analytic Strategy and Lifecycle Management Predictive models can anticipate the likelihood of a person to respond to an offer, or respond to an offer within a particular channel. Coupled with customer segmentation strategies, models can help you focus on groups of "like" people—understanding and anticipating their behavior and facilitating the tailoring of messaging and content instead of taking a one-size-fits-all approach. Model scores, represented as a percentage likelihood to respond to a given event or fit a various profile, and model algorithms driving decisions at the point of interaction can be integrated within a business rules or decision management architecture.

Enterprise Decision Capabilities Hub The decision hub sits at the center of the ecosystem and directs traffic across an automated business decisioning processes. This is the technology hub that integrates operational and analytic decisions by integrating applications, workflow, business rules, and analytics. In addition to customer offer eligibility rules and models, pricing, underwriting, and fraud detection models can be layered into the process.

Data Strategy and Platform Architecture Of course, none of this is possible without data. Ideally, you have this perfect database with a complete view of the customer and everything you want to know about them in one place. Unfortunately, that's just not a reality for many organizations. But don't fear—many organizations take an incremental approach to getting out of product silos and into a customer-centric data view. However, the need for customer data integration becomes more critical as the organization moves toward automated decisioning processes and the number of channels increase.

KPI (Key Performance Indicators)—Measurement and Monitoring Every initiative must be measured. Without clear and consistent metrics there will be a lack of accountability for your strategy. This leads to an inability to accurately measure new test-and-learn approaches to improve results. Key questions asked are: How do we measure the success of our program? What metrics drive accountability? How do we incentivize our resources? Consistent and credible metrics are essential to organizational buy-in. They also provide an indicator of when the organization needs to readjust the strategy.

This integrated data-driven approach creates relevancy for your customers at the point of interaction:

> *Bank of America launched their BankAmeriDeals loyalty program in 2012. The program mines transactions in their customers' bank accounts to see what purchases they make, and sends them offers from other merchants that complement those purchases. Since the program launch, Bank of America has sent out more than 1.5 billion offers across their more than 40 million online and mobile banking customers. In a unique twist, the customer activates the discount online (web or mobile), uses their bankcard to make a purchase, and then receives cash back in their bank account. The bank estimates that they've saved customers $20 million since the program launch and that the program positively impacts customer retention.*[3]

OUR EXAMPLE IN MOTION

As we start down the path to creating our customer-centric analytic hub, we'll use a hypothetical company to illustrate the real-world opportunities and challenges faced by most organizations, and to

---

[3] Heather Fletcher, "Cover Story: First Date, Sans Coupons," *Target Marketing* (February 1, 2014).

provide an agile framework that you can use to manage through these challenges. The example will reflect a collection of experiences and practices leveraged by many companies, large and small, analytically immature and mature, gathered from companies we've worked with over the past few years. Our hypothetical company, Always Best Products, Inc. (ABP), reflects many of these organizations: They have analytic capabilities and some great talent, but the overall organization has been slow to adopt analytics within the day-to-day cycle of the business. Out of necessity, our analytic team has been managing all things analytics alone, with little support from IT. After reaching critical mass, they undertake an initiative to improve engagement, execution, and delivery by implementing an agile framework. Throughout this book, we'll follow ABP's journey on a high-profile analytic project that crosses business, operational, and technological boundaries.

ENABLING INNOVATION

Transformation is always disruptive. The organizational change required in the standardization and integration process requires reconfiguration of roles and responsibilities, the design or redesign of business processes, and the implementation, integration, and rationalization of technology platforms—and we need new, more efficient ways of accomplishing this! Analytics, in the form of predictive algorithms, propensity scores, segments, and so on, are integrated within the business processes. The need for the analytic teams to modernize and integrate within this ecosystem is critical.

The organization must develop the ability to modularize the components of business processes. Automated decisioning workflows must be flexible enough to be reconfigured easily, allowing for changes and enhancements, whether to the process itself, the analytic components within the process, or new technologies. For many organizations, this requires rethinking their solution delivery models. IT departments typically have mature delivery capabilities around their operational systems. However, the integration of data, new technologies, and analytic methods requires a new iterative delivery rhythm as you try different customer treatments and approaches—you're not always going to know what works! This ability to integrate trial-and-error analytics into the process may be challenging to both IT departments and analytic teams!

While it may sound daunting, there are pragmatic approaches to increasing capabilities in all of these areas and incrementally developing the organizational and technology frameworks to enable them. Few companies have mastered all elements of this vision—the first step is to frame out the vision, identify your current capabilities, prioritize your high-impact opportunities, and test and learn along the way.

CHAPTER 2

The Analytic Lifecycle

A nalytics is an ambiguous and overused term that carries different meanings across business stakeholder communities, technology organizations, and analytic teams. An important starting point for creating a more data-driven culture is to define a common language around it. The common language creates a shared understanding within the organization and helps clarify roles and responsibilities. Once this has been established, it becomes simpler to frame out analytic projects. One tool that can be useful in this process is the analytic value chain, which provides a structure for incorporating analytic projects within a broader business ecosystem. In the center of the value chain sits the analytic development lifecycle (ALDC). The six-stage ADLC approach helps organizations better align to business strategies by identifying engagement points across the stakeholder communities.

WHAT ARE ANALYTICS, ANYWAY?

In many organizations, analytics plays an integral role in the enterprise decision-making process. Credit card companies decide whether to issue you a credit card, and insurers decide whether to issue you a policy—and at what cost! E-tailers anticipate what other products you might like to buy or what coupons and discounts you might respond to. Digital media services predict what movies and music you might like based on "people like you." More and more, analytics help our organizations make good, profitable decisions that keep customers happy.

Here's where things start to get messy: The term *analytics* has become so overused that it's meaning has become lost—or at the very least, it means a lot of different things to different people. Different organizations are at different analytic maturity phases: For some organizations, their analytic baseline might still focus on rear-view mirror analysis and reporting; for others, they're generating dozens (or hundreds!) of predictive models a day; and even more sophisticated companies may be automating their business decisioning processes through artificial intelligence and other machine learning engines

However, the term *advanced analytics* needs clarification, as it is often poorly understood. Organizations are asking: What separates "advanced" from non-advanced? What exactly is data mining, machine learning, or big data? Is there a difference between business intelligence and advanced analytics? Who are data scientists, and what do they do? There is a logical reason for this confusion: It means different things to different companies, functions, departments, and projects, and all of the noise in the marketplace and media doesn't help. While the output of analytics varies, the ability to use data to better understand and positively influence your customers and business environment, create new innovative products, or simply make better operational decisions is the common denominator.

With the importance of analytics in the context and continuum of enterprise decision-making (as illustrated in Figure 2.1), our focus will be on forward-looking analytics—anticipating, influencing, and optimizing through the use of predictive models, segments, or scores that drive a specific outcome. Rear-view mirror analytics—reporting and analysis, as examples—are essential in monitoring the performance of your business strategy, uncovering new trends, and evaluating predictive model performance. While an analytics strategy is pointless without measurement, our focus on the reporting aspects of analytics will only be as an output of the predictive modeling process.

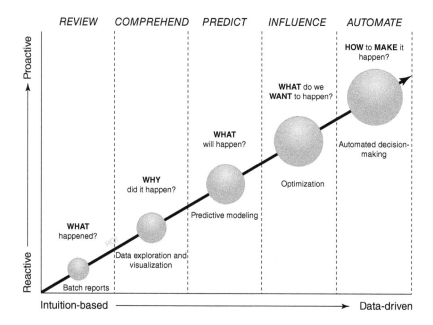

Figure 2.1 Analytic ROI Model

ANALYTICS IN YOUR ORGANIZATION

The use of analytics ranges from company to company. Companies with deep pockets may have big, well-established analytics teams with over a hundred data scientists. Other research divisions are, in essence, a shop of one. Others may use consultants or outsourcing partners to drive their analytic programs. And still many other companies are at the starting point of this journey, contemplating analytics and understanding where it fits in their business.

The good news is that for most organizations, the value of analytics is no longer in question. The ubiquity of data and tools to analyze information means that analytics no longer needs to be locked into a centralized department of PhDs and quants. Analytics cuts across departments and functions; it crosses divisions and transcends hierarchical levels. Market leaders embed analytics as the strategic value in the culture of the company where decision-making is data-driven or at least guided by data, and innovation and efficiency is derived or optimized by the widespread use of analytics by any number of users.

Wherever you may be on the maturity curve, the spectrum of analytics at your disposal might include a variety of tools and techniques used for basic reporting and visualization all the way to statistical modeling, forecasting, and optimization. But even with the level of organizational awareness of analytics increasing, most analytic teams are still operating outside the bounds of the organization. As a result, these teams often don't get the necessary business and IT support needed to work effectively.

Even more challenging, the technology ecosystem surrounding analytics grows more complex by the day: New data technologies, processing capabilities, analytic programming languages and tools, and cloud-based computing options simultaneously open doors for analysts, but increase the complexity of managing and keeping pace with the tools and technologies. Analysts comfortable with working data on their desktop may be confounded by the plethora of analytic applications, data platforms, and security and governance requirements. Now, more than ever, analytic teams need the broader support of their organizations.

Analytic teams must strengthen ties and partner with IT. There is always the inclination to want to fly solo. The analytic teams think that IT interferes with their ability to be agile, and in many companies they do! The downside is that your analysts end up creating (and living with the aftermath of) data structures never meant to be put into production, as well as trying to maintain operational modeling and reporting processes. They often lack the skills and discipline to create and maintain the data and technology infrastructure and end up doing it poorly, or find themselves hiring shadow IT resources to help them operate under the covers. This might be acceptable in certain situations, but enterprise decision support requires IT horsepower. What's needed is a new engagement model that supports all sides of the analytic process.

The implementation considerations are equally daunting. If you're going to use analytics to drive change in a business-critical enterprise decisioning process, a lot of thought has to go into how the data and model are structured, validated, and deployed in an operational environment. Since IT often hasn't been engaged in the analytic development process, they are naturally suspicious of the analytic team's "process" since it likely doesn't conform to IT implementation standards.

CASE STUDY EXAMPLE

One large healthcare organization was faced with a significant challenge. Fraudulent health claims remain a challenge for the industry. The problem was so important that the company dedicated a data scientist team to tackling fraud detection. Over a three-year period, the team created several models to identify fraudulent claims at the start of the claims process. When a claimant filed a claim, the claims administration system triggered a score on the claim and either fast-tracked for payment or sent to a triage unit for further investigation.

While the statistical skill of the scientists or validity of the models was never in question, IT found it nearly impossible to translate the analytic models into the programming languages and structure needed by the operational claims environment. Their analytic lifecycle process—creating a new predictive model and moving it from development to deployment—was taking almost two years. The process of reevaluating and refreshing models in production could take close to a year. The IT department needed close to a dozen full-time programmers to recode the data workflows and predictive models into IT standard tools, languages, and applications. The annual development cost exceeded $2 million.

The problem grew so severe that it became an organizational priority to fix it. During the discovery process, they uncovered manual

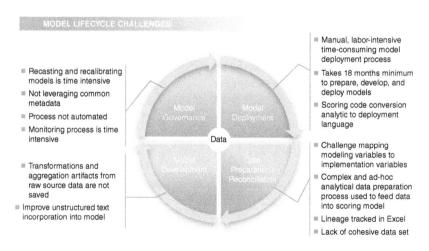

Figure 2.2 Analytic Lifecycle Challenges Identified in a Healthcare Organization

processes, lack of standardization (tools, techniques, processes) across the data scientist team, and poorly documented code and data sources. Figure 2.2 highlights these challenges.

The problems faced by this healthcare company are fairly common across all industries. As we go through this book, these are the challenges that we'll help all parts of the organization—business, IT, and analytics groups—address.

BEYOND IT: THE BUSINESS ANALYTIC VALUE CHAIN

Beyond the technology conundrum, analytics form part of a broader business value chain. Analytics change and improve your business, so you can't just think about insights and models and scores in a vacuum. They need to be considered within a broader business and technology framework.

The analytic lifecycle drives business process improvement and business enablement, resulting in strategic value to the organization (see Figure 2.3). The lifecycle is aligned to a broader business strategy where analytics are strategically managed within a portfolio, so the

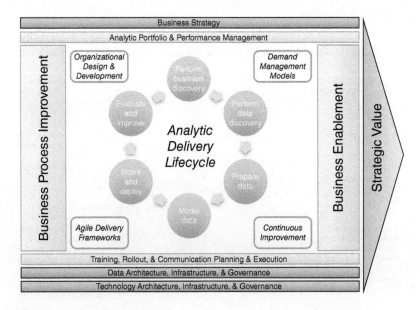

Figure 2.3 Analytic Value Chain

analytic effort is focused and aligned. Critical analytic foundations include the data and technology platforms supporting the analytics, as well as training, change management, and communication strategies. Good analytics change your business!

The key message is that analytic teams don't work in isolation. They're part of a broader business ecosystem. Organizations need a more formal structure or discipline to support and create analytics. In the following chapters, we'll show you some methods, tools, and techniques that you can employ in your business analytic projects that respect the creative process, but also provide some structure to analytic process modernization.

ANALYTIC DELIVERY LIFECYCLE

Our analytic value chain revolves around an iterative lifecycle characterized by six stages (see Figure 2.4). Not all analytic projects result in a deployable predictive model or algorithm, but all analytic work encompasses the first three stages. As business conditions change and new data, technologies, or methodologies become available, analysts may iterate through different stages of the cycle on a continuous basis. Let's review the stages at a high level.

Figure 2.4 Analytic Delivery Lifecycle

Stage One—Perform Business Discovery

With the exception of machine learning techniques, all analytics start with a business question, issue, or objective. Analysts may be asked to explore a certain area of the business to help guide or define a business strategy, or the organization may be ready to embed models (i.e., propensity to buy, pricing, etc.) into an operational system. Regardless, as the team is starting out, exploratory sessions are held to define the business opportunity and identify starting points: What behavior do we need to influence or predict with our model? What data support the analysis? Where are the data? Is the project viable? Through the process, the analyst may uncover additional opportunities for analysis, gaps in understanding that can be clarified, or gaps in data.

A great first step in this process is to hold a discovery workshop. Identify and include the relevant business stakeholders. Using interview and facilitation techniques, learn from the business what they think is behind the problem they're looking to solve. For example, let's say that a business is seeing an increase in customer churn.

The business stakeholders get together in the discovery session to discuss what they believe is behind the increase:

- The product team believes that decline in retention rates is due to the organization's product structure. Competitors are coming out with similar offerings that are packaged differently and may be more appealing to customers.

- The customer service believes that inflexible payment options are contributing to the decline.

- Marketing believes that customers don't understand the value proposition. They've also done demographic research that shows that there is declining demand for their product overall due to demographic changes.

For the analyst, this process helps guide them in terms of different business questions to analyze (i.e., what is the effect of pricing changes on retention?) and guide them to the data needed to answer those questions.

Stage Two—Perform Data Discovery

Data come in many forms: structured or unstructured, categorical or numeric, aggregated or transactional, longitudinal or latitudinal, and on and on. In most organizations, data lives both internally and externally across a variety of platforms. You'll find data in centralized data sets or data warehouses, spreadsheets, applications, service representative notes, social media feeds, third-party data sources, emails, and service calls (speech-to-text). It's not just the raw data that's important, but the variables that analysts can derive from the data.

A challenge faced by analysts is that certain data sources are under lock and key. Some data sources by nature of their sensitivity (such as personal data) must be carefully governed; some data elements can't be used in certain modeling scenarios (such as using ethnographic details to determine credit scores); and some are nonsensitive, but under the domain of data gatekeepers.

As you're identifying data sources that are appropriate for your project, you'll have to find those data owners—the people in your company that can not only give you access to the data but also help you interpret its business context. Also of consideration are the hidden costs to gathering data. Most operational data sources aren't structured appropriately for modeling. There may be issues with completeness, quality, and interpretation. In some cases, it may be better to start with what's readily available and then phase in additional data sources over time.

Many companies operate under the assumption that before they can perform any advanced analytic work, they need to create an all-encompassing, one-source-of-truth data warehouse. The reality is that most data warehouses will never be able to keep up with the needs of the analytic team, and a new way must be found to supporting those needs.

During the modeling process, each business issue or question may require a different data perspective or structure. Thinking that one source will solve all needs is unrealistic. On the flipside, you don't want the analytics group building its own secret data warehouse that lives on a computer under somebody's desk.

If you're just getting started, start with what you know. The company with the retention problem we outlined in the previous section knew a lot about their data sources as they related to their operational systems. What they uncovered during the data discovery process is that the data were not well suited for analytic work. There were many errors and exceptions in the data, as well as inconsistent application of business rules. As the data sources were aggregated and transformed for the segmentation and modeling work, the business teams came back together to agree on the logic that would be used to clean and prepare the data. The logic and the data sources were documented as part of the project's artifacts.

Stage Three—Prepare Data

Once data are gathered, the next step is to clean, prepare, and explore the data. If you're working with new data sources, this can be a valuable step for the analyst to better understand the data. Too often, modelers or analysts are anxious to get right into the data and start modeling or looking for trends and patterns, often skipping over the most important step in the process—comprehending the data.

During the data exploration stage, the modeler begins to better understand the data and the relationship between the variables. This process encourages dialogue with subject matter experts and allows the modeler to make good decisions on how to structure the data set. It is through this process that creative juices begin to flow and ideas come about in creating new variables.

In this stage of work, data are parsed, collapsed, scrubbed, and manipulated. Exploratory techniques using descriptive statistics such as histograms, two-way frequencies, heat maps, and others help to uncover opportunities to create new variables or reconfigure the data set. The exploration and preparation phase generates a lot of business insight, revelations, and patterns. In fact, your business stakeholders may find the output of this phase more valuable than the actual modeling results. Many analytic projects are completed in the data exploration stage. For others, a model is the end goal and they move on to the next stage of the analytic lifecycle.

Expect that this stage in the analytic lifecycle will consume the majority of your resource time on new projects. For ongoing model development and refinement, it is important to have a model-ready data set that is derived from the raw data that are well documented and coded clearly and maintained for future updates to the model.

Stage Four—Model Data

Once a modeling data set has been created, analysts can choose from any number of applications, programming languages, and statistical modeling methodologies to start their work. In general, some problems are better suited to certain tools or techniques, but most analysts will use a wide range of methods in the model development process. As noted in the previous step, it's usually not the methodology or the software that is the differentiator, but the quality data used as an input.

If you have a bunch of modelers each with different software and they are given the same data set and asked to create a model using the same variables, the models will come out fairly equal in terms of predictive power regardless of the methodology or software that they use. If the modelers are allowed to create new variables or find new sources of data, that is when you will find differentiation in the quality and predictive power of the models.

Models may be used to simply identify key factors in a process or may be used as a tool to enable more efficiency and automation or better decision-making. If data is available to analyze, then those factors can be quantified and used as model inputs. The beauty of models is that they are unbiased (to the extent of the data), consistent, and holistic in nature. This enables us to consider many factors all at once rather than one factor at a time.

Some modelers like to have lots of variables in their models. It gives them a false blanket of security. With too many variables comes another issue: implementation challenges. The number of variables in a model is positively correlated with a probability of error in scoring and deploying the model. There may be operational issues in deploying a model with a large number of variables if there are system performance requirements or operational system limitations. Finally, models with too many variables can be difficult to explain to business stakeholders. As part of your deployment strategy, you might consider models that have similar lift to your "winning" model, but with fewer variables.

Stage Five—Score and Deploy

If your model scores or algorithms are going to be deployed in an operational environment, it is important to work closely with IT throughout the project. The ADLC may not be synched to a traditional software development lifecycle that IT departments are comfortable with (or operational systems are aligned to). The iterative nature of the ADLC and the (perceived or real) lack of controls and standardization cause headaches, consternation, and downright fear in most IT organizations.

Model inputs and derived variables in the model need to be sourced appropriate to minimize the corruption of data. The analytics team must audit the implementation with test cases to ensure calculations, which are often time dependent and complex, are accurate. The data sources need to be stabilized to ensure the consistency and accuracy of the data.

Although an audit captures the majority of coding errors, it is difficult to audit every possible situation. Monitoring input data and profiling derived data and scores also help to spot errors or changes in the data. For example, in one organization, the IT department closely audited a model. During the audit process, an astute IT programmer noted that some of the raw data was missing for a particular variable. The IT programmer followed standard data protocol and recoded missing values as "0." Unfortunately, the "missing" value was a predictor in the model. The misinterpretation was not discovered until several months into deployment and the model was missing about 10 percent of its target records. After research and review of the coding, the "error" was ultimately discovered and corrected.

A similar example involved a third-party data vendor that started recoding nulls as "0" in their data. This change was found within a week when the monitoring report flagged the variable with a significant profile change. This change, however, required rework to the model.

It is also a good idea to create a standardized preaudited test data set that may be run through the model on a daily or weekly basis, to ensure that the scoring algorithm is intact and working correctly.

Stage Six—Evaluate and Improve

Before the model is deployed, it is important to establish a monitoring system of the raw data flowing into the model, the derivations of the variable values, and the actual calculation of the score to ensure the model's ongoing integrity. Profiling the score distribution is also helpful to see if the population is drifting over time.

Models often need updating annually and possibly more frequently if the environment is changing rapidly or if the target audience has changed. There are two types of model updates. One update revolves around a simple data refresh, in which the variables in the model are not changed but more current data are used to refresh the coefficients of the variables in the model. The second type of model update, which is more time consuming, involves a complete rebuild in which all the variables from the modeling data set are reconsidered with the potential for the variables in the model to change.

Most importantly, the model needs to be reviewed for efficacy. Is it doing what we wanted it do? Is it indeed finding the most profitable customers, increasing revenue, or reducing the error rate? Some outcomes have longer tails or take more time to develop, such as liability insurance claims. Even in those situations, you need to develop proxies or interim measures that may be used to calculate the cost/benefit and or added value of the model.

GETTING STARTED

Good analytic execution requires a disciplined approach to not only the model development process, but also the integration within the broader business and technology landscape. In the business context, if analytics are not done correctly, a really good model will sit on the shelf collecting dust either because the business customer did not buy-in, there was effective resistance or even sabotage by the end users, or errors were made when implementing the model. Whatever, the reason, the end result is the same—missed value in influencing the business objective of sales, profits, reduced costs, and so on. Even worse, it could make future analytic projects much more difficult to get funding for.

SUMMARY

While analytics are becoming more mainstream, there's still a wide range of organizational maturity in defining analytics and being able to leverage that insight into business decision-making processes. The technology landscape is growing more complex every day as new software applications, programming languages, and database platforms emerge. Environmental changes, in the form of information security procedures, are also impacting how analysts perform their work today. As a result, the analytic organization of today needs to be much more engaged with their business and technology partners. Analysts follow a six-stage analytic development process that integrates with the organization's analytic value chain—a flow of insight that influences business and technology decision processes. Analytic teams need to modernize their processes and practices to work effectively in this new world.

CHAPTER **3**

Getting Your Analytic Project off the Ground

egardless of whether your organization is analytically nascent or mature, engaging with your business stakeholders is the best place to start. Even in analytically mature companies, different functional areas within the business may need assistance in defining and prioritizing their analytic projects. To help illustrate our point, we'll follow a hypothetical company with very common challenges through an analytic project. In our narrative, Isabel, our lead data scientist at ADP, is having a conversation with Sherry, the vice president of the call center. Sherry's group has noted a significant decline in customer retention and believes that analytics can help them solve the problem. Isabel engages with Sherry's team to better understand the business problem they're trying to solve, and helps them craft a vision for solving it.

Figure 3.1 illustrates the process that the team goes through in the visioning process.

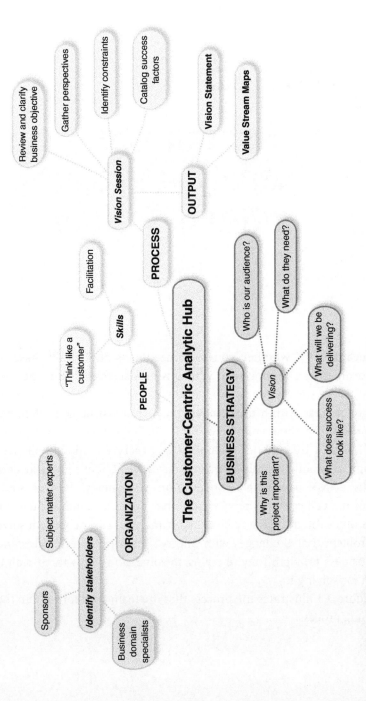

Figure 3.1 The Customer-Centric Analytic Hub Visioning Considerations

A DAY IN THE LIFE

Our lead data scientist, Isabel, comes into the office, and before going to her desk she takes a look at the team's task board to get an up-to-date status on their work in progress. Her team is working on several strategic projects at the moment, and the board gives her a current view of what work's been accomplished and what's outstanding. While most of the team's work supports the marketing department's customer acquisition and cross-sell initiatives, they also take on analytic projects across the organization. Since marketing has been using analytics for some time, they have an established process for requesting and completing work that works well for both groups. Other parts of the organization have less maturity around analytics.

Later that morning, Isabel receives an email from Sherry, the vice president of the call center. They've noticed a decrease in their customer retention numbers and want to find out if the analytic team can help solve their business problem. The call center hasn't used predictive models to support their operations before. As Isabel sits down with Sherry, she discovers that her understanding of "analytics" is pretty low. She's also having trouble articulating what the specific business problem is. In the back of her mind, Isabel is thinking about the data: She knows that the call center data sources are different from the sources the team typically uses. The call center also has its own dedicated IT department—the data sciences team hasn't worked with them either.

> "Since we're losing more customers than we've planned for in our operating budget, this project is of the highest priority," Sherry tells her. "We have the CEO's support on doing whatever it takes to move the needle in the opposite direction."

Isabel thinks for a minute. The data sciences team has a lot of work on their plate right now. Before jumping into the project, she suggests getting a group of stakeholders together for a visioning session to better understand what the organization believes is causing the problem. This will help ensure everyone starts off on the same page and give us the inputs we need to prioritize the work, Isabel tells Sherry. She agrees.

> Isabel goes back to her desk and calls Rebecca, the project coordinator for the data sciences team. "I've got a great

project," Isabel says, "but I need some help scoping it out and prioritizing it against all the other stuff we have going on. I met with Sherry, the VP, and suggested that we move forward with a visioning session so that we can understand the scope of the problem and its importance to the organization."

VISIONING

Establishing a project vision is a critical component of the project initiation process. The vision provides the overarching goal that aligns the project team to the importance of the work, and helps create a shared understanding of the overall objectives of the project from both an organizational and customer perspective. The session helps the team outline what the business believes to be the core drivers of the problem, as it provides a good starting point for analysis.

> Rebecca calls Sherry: "I'm setting up the vision session for the retention project. Who should be invited to the session? Typically we like to have representation from people who understand the business as well as your technology partners. Let me share a little on how the process works ... "
>
> Sherry provides Rebecca with a list of attendees and Rebecca reaches out to them. She sets up a two hour scoping session. Sherry thinks a full-day session would be better. "Let's start with a focused two-hour session," Rebecca replies, "we need just enough information to start shaping the problem. If additional sessions are needed, we can continue the discussions—we actually try not to gather every single bit of information up front. As we move forward with the project, we can discuss the best ways to work together."
>
> "Well," Sherry answers, "my team's time is really tight. I was hoping we could provide you with all the information up front and then your team could just go do the work."
>
> "It's really important that your team stays actively engaged throughout the project," Rebecca says. "Once we go through the visioning session and the project is prioritized, we'll work together to define the project team and the time commitments."

"Okay," responds Sherry, unconvinced. "But what do we get out of the session? In our IT projects we create a project charter. Is this the same thing?"

"Sort of," says Rebecca. "A vision statement is typically a one-page document that helps clarify the work to be done—it's a great communication tool. It's short and sweet and tells a story."

A good vision statement communicates the purpose and value of the project. It provides team members with direction and shapes customer understanding. For those familiar with traditional project management methodologies, a critical difference between a vision statement and a project charter is that the vision statement is not a formal contract. The vision statement provides a clear and concise definition of the goal of the project and what success means. It's enough information for sponsors and stakeholders to make organizational decisions on cost, time, and scope, but at the same time it acknowledges that those inputs may change as the project progresses.

While it might be tempting to skip over this step, it is critical for providing the foundation for the project as it sets boundaries and aligns expectations across the stakeholder groups. As we start to move into an agile framework, the vision statement, like all agile documentation, should align with the concept of being "minimally sufficient." The primary value of capturing the vision occurs in the dialogues between stakeholders, not the actual document itself.

Your vision statement can be summarized as follows:

The vision statement doesn't expressly specify how this will be accomplished, but frames the problem statement in terms of a business goal. The "how" would be captured in the requirements. Typically, the project sponsors will be responsible for owning the vision statement

Table 3.1 Vision Statement Template

Vision Statement: Summarize the project vision or idea			
Audience	Needs	Product	Success Factors
Which population are we targeting and why?	What are the needs of our customers? What are the needs of the organization?	What will we be delivering?	How will the work benefit our customers and our organization? What metrics can we use to define success?

(see Table 3.1) and retain responsibility for ensuring that the vision is well understood by the organization, internal and external stakeholders, and the project team. The vision statement is iterative, and the project team has input into shaping the final vision for the project.

FACILITATING YOUR VISIONING SESSION

Like anything else, facilitation is a skill. The facilitator's responsibility is to ensure that the group's time is spent productively by achieving the meeting's objectives. Rebecca has a diverse group coming to the visioning session—the team members are coming from different functional areas and are at different organizational levels. She's pretty sure that many of the participants don't know each other and is concerned that senior level people may dominate the conversation.

In advance of the meeting, Rebecca sends out an email with an agenda outlining objectives, expectations, and desired outcomes. She includes an overview of the business issue that they're there to discuss and its importance to the organization. Behind the scenes, Rebecca prepares a list of topics in advance, so they group can focus on what's important. Her agenda includes:

- A review and clarification of the business objective to gain business understanding. This portion of the meeting can include capturing how the business operates, which is especially important if the analytic team does not have domain expertise. Remember, the objective is to gather just enough information. If you uncover gaps in understanding during the session, schedule follow-ups to clarify.

- Once the objective is clarified, gather perspectives on what stakeholders believe is causing the issue. The step helps to identify boundaries as well as identifies additional areas that could possibly be influenced.

- Identify current organizational constraints. Don't spend too much time here. If your stakeholders are too focused on constraints, then they won't be open to a wider range of solutions.

You want to keep everyone away from "We can't do that because of XYZ … " conversations.

- Catalog success factors for the initiative. What would success look like? Is there any way to tell what "done" looks like?

THINK LIKE A CUSTOMER

All too often, we take an inside-out perspective. What this means is that we see a customer's journey from how we engage with them as a company, not how they engage with us as a consumer. A helpful tool in identifying how customers engage with us is by creating a customer journey map (see Figure 3.2). The journey map helps identify all the paths customers take in achieving their goals from start to finish. By looking at your organization through your customers' eyes, you can begin to better understand the challenges that a customer faces in doing business with your organization. The team sees the customer outside of product or functional silos and helps link pieces of a customer process across the organization. Often, teams find that potential solutions for the problems that they're identifying extend outside of their functional realms—and that's okay!

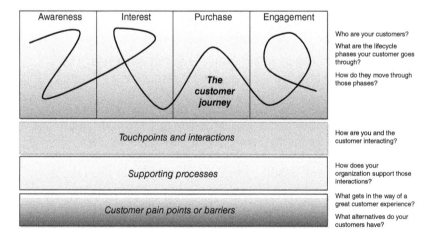

Figure 3.2 Customer Journey Map

In the visioning session with the call center and technology teams, the group outlines a typical customer day-in-the-life:

> The call center lead pipes up: "I keep hearing from our customers that we don't have enough flexible payment options—but our competitors do!"
>
> And an other call center representative: "We don't have a customer lifecycle. Either someone is a customer or not. Our current approach is to treat everyone the same."
>
> And another: "We don't do a good enough job at positioning the value of our products."
>
> From the IT corner: "We're in the process of putting in a new customer relationship management system. Won't that solve our problems?"
>
> Wow, that's a lot of information. The scope of this problem is bigger than I thought! Rebecca thinks. Isabel is looking nervous—this project is clearly poorly defined. She's coming across a problem that's common—the problem expands beyond the group that is charged with fixing the issue. "Okay, that's great information," she says, "let's start brainstorming all the reasons that we think cause customers to leave." Once we have that, she muses, we can start to map out a customer lifecycle, create the customer journey map, and identify different points that we might be able to influence with analytics.
>
> Rebecca begins to flesh out the vision statement. "All right team, give me some insight on our current retention opportunity." Sherry pulls out a report: "We forecasted a overall customer retention rate of 75 percent. We defined a retained customer as someone who buys an additional product no more than six months after his or her last purchase. Over the past six months, our retention rate has been declining steadily. At this rate, we'll finish the year at 65 percent, which will significantly impact our bottom line."
>
> "That's a great place to start," says Rebecca. "How's this for our vision statement: To retain high value and profitable customers with a goal of meeting or exceeding our 75 percent retention threshold over the next 12 months."

"That sounds fine," says Sherry, "but we don't really know who's profitable. Our metric is based on the number of people that we retain, not how profitable they are."

Sensing some tension from the group, Rebecca writes customer profitability in the parking lot space on the whiteboard. "It's important," she says, "but obviously not your primary focus area today. We'll table it for now and see if it's feasible to incorporate down the road. Just keep in mind that our vision statement gives us a starting point, not an end point."

By the end of the meeting, Rebecca and Isabel have a good understanding of the business problem and they have enough information to present to the executive committee for prioritization. At this early stage of the project, the focus will be on understanding the influencing factors that make people leave. Since the outcome of an analytic project is often ambiguous, the group decides that the first step will be to perform an analysis of the available data in order to identify variables that influence retention.

As you facilitate your vision session, keep your stakeholders from doing too much problem solving. See Table 3.2 for an example. Since business problems such as customer retention are far reaching throughout the organization, don't let your participants wander down rabbit holes. Keep people focused on the task at hand. Depending on the business problem you're working on, crafting your vision statement will likely take more than one session.

Table 3.2 Vision Statement

Vision Statement: To retain customers with a goal of meeting or exceeding our 75 percent retention threshold over the next 12 months.				
Business Problem	**Audience**	**Focus Area**	**Product**	**Success Factors**
Over the past six months, our retention rate has been declining steadily. At the current run rate, we'll finish the year at 65% of customers retained, which will significantly impact our bottom line.	The initial focus of the analysis will be on people that haven't bought any additional products in the six-month period after their initial purchase.	What are the influencing factors that make people leave?	Analysis of available data to identify variables that influence retention	Meet or exceed the 75% retention threshold over the next 12 months.

SUMMARY

As the team comes together and begins to scope out their project, they start with the creation of the vision statement. The purpose of the vision statement is to create a shared understanding of the business opportunity that can be communicated across different levels of the organization. For an agile project, the vision statement is used to initiate the project. As an input into the visioning process, the team may want to create a customer journey map to organize the information about the customer relationship. The journey map can provide insights into some of the root causes of the analytic problem that you're looking at. As an output of the visioning session, the analytic team works with the business customer to develop a project vision statement that can be used as an input into prioritization. The vision statement includes a purpose statement, identification of the target, the needs of the organization, what the project may deliver, and the value of the project to the organization. In our project, the vision statement is used as a communication tool for the executive steering committee, who will determine if the team should continue to move forward with the project.

CHAPTER 4

Project Justification and Prioritization

n data-intensive businesses, information needs across the organization are high. Teams supporting analytic initiatives often struggle to achieve strategic analytic goals while managing day-to-day tactical requests. A formal demand management mechanism helps balance tactical and strategic delivery. An important component of prioritizing the analytic initiative lies in understanding its value to the organization. While some companies may set aside budgets for innovation projects, most organizations need to balance innovation with other work at hand. Value- and financial-based prioritization methods help teams quantify and qualify that value.

ORGANIZATIONAL VALUE OF ANALYTICS

Most analytic teams provide a "free" service to their organization, making it difficult to quantify the value of the team and to effectively prioritize the analytic requests that come into the team. Analytic teams have long resisted the business chargeback models employed by IT because they believe that it gives them agility and flexibility in supporting their business partners. The upside is that this is true; the downside is that this can result in chaos—since there is no effective cost to a project or ways to identify trade-offs in completing one project over another, the team lacks any ability to prioritize their work and ensure that their resources are deployed on high value projects.

An inability to say no to business customers also results in resources performing tasks that may not be well aligned to their skillset. For example, let's say one of your data scientists completed a project for a business unit. That business partner was really happy, and now calls that data scientist for every informational request that they have. The data scientist finds herself running reports and pulling data to support the requests, but now doesn't have the time to take on any analytic project work. She gets frustrated because she's not doing the work she's trained to do, and then she quits. It happens all the time.

Another challenge in this situation is that it is difficult to institutionalize any of the analytic output. The process that each analyst uses in the creation of his or her analysis is unique. The resources become such specialists that they end up being bottlenecks: No one else on the team knows the process or system for getting work done.

In a worst-case scenario, a business customer may make the same request of multiple people on the team to see who can get the work done the fastest. The team members aren't talking to each other, so no one knows that they're all doing the same work. And yes, this happens all the time, too! Not only is this a terrible waste of resources and talent but also team members are likely to come up with different answers to the problem, requiring additional time spent justifying the results.

The good news is that you can overcome these challenges, but it does require strong leadership (and retraining your business customers!).

ANALYTIC DEMAND MANAGEMENT STRATEGY

In fact, one organization exactly faced the challenges outlined above. As part of an organizational transformation, it completely overhauled its business intelligence and analytics (BI&A) delivery model.

The first change made was to shift alignment of the BI&A team. The team formerly reported to the finance organization, but had responsibility for supporting the entire division. Not surprisingly, finance-related analytic projects were always a priority. In the new model, the BI&A team reported to the divisional president; this gave them an equal seat at the table with the other functional areas.

The second change was the team's funding model. The other functional areas would pay for the team's budget. The budget included money for resources and a pool of funding for strategic projects. Recognizing the need to "keep the lights on" for tactical day-to-day requests, the leadership team agreed that 40 percent of the overall budget would be allocated to tactical requests and 60 percent to strategic projects. In addition to full-time staff, the budget supported contract and offshore delivery resources.

In turn, the business would get to participate in the project prioritization process (strategic and tactical), and receive a full accounting of how the overall budget was being allocated. To support the prioritization process, the organization established a two-tiered governance system with a triage process for requests and enhancements, as shown in Figure 4.1.

The Business as Partners: Committee Structure

Executive Committee—Senior level guidance to:
- Set priorities for achieving organizational analytic and data driven strategies.
- Resolve and set direction on competing priorities.
- Ensure that projects achieve analytic goals.

Working Group Committee—Partnership with analytic stakeholders to:
- Hands-on management/participation within the strategic analytic program.
- Initiate and prioritize information requests.
- Identify priority issues to escalate to executive committee.

Analytic Team—Facilitation and execution:
- Facilitate the information gathering and delivery process.
- Develop solution direction and boundaries.
- Project execution and management.

Figure 4.1 Business as Partners

Executive Steering Committee The steering committee comprises senior-level management with representation across each functional area of the business. The steering committee is accountable for determining the overall funding of the BI&A organization, and prioritization and oversight of the strategic BI&A portfolio of work. The steering committee meets on a monthly basis.

Working Committee Mid-level managers make up the working committee, each responsible for representing their functional area's needs. The working committee delegate serves as a gatekeeper for their business unit. They are accountable for the requests from their area and submit them as appropriate to the BI&A team.

Triage Process The BI&A team then triages the request: If something can be completed within a certain time frame (i.e., less than six hours), the request is completed. If it will take longer, it goes to the working committee for prioritization. If there is a conflict over prioritization, it can be escalated to the steering committee for resolution. If the work effort exceeded a certain threshold, the request had to be prioritized by the working committee. The request owner would present a business case, and the committee would vote on where it fit in the prioritization matrix. Any request that had not yet been started could be reprioritized.

As you can imagine, an engagement model like this requires a lot of top-down support and discipline to be successful. One of the agreements made by the leadership team is that all analytic resources would be concentrated within the BI&A team. This strategy was intended to keep the business units from creating their own shadow analytic teams. However, as organizations grow in size, a centralized analytic team may become a bottleneck. In this case, it might make more sense to decentralize the resources, but coordinate them through a "center of excellence" type model where standards are defined and governed, but execution happens locally (see Figure 4.2).

RESULTS

Because the BI&A team had executive support, the new governance model worked extremely well. The functional teams were able to get work done in a democratic way. The prioritization process helped the

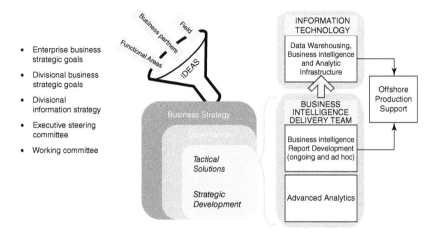

- Enterprise business strategic goals
- Divisional business strategic goals
- Divisional information strategy
- Executive steering committee
- Working committee

Figure 4.2 BI&A Demand Management Model

entire group take a more organizational-centric view, by aligning their requests with enterprise and divisional business strategies. The team's capacity to work on larger strategic projects increased dramatically. In fact, the earliest strategic projects focused on creating self-service capabilities for the functional areas, so they could begin to answer their own business questions, freeing up even more capacity.

The hardest part about implementing a model like this is the business change management. The BI&A team needed to create a governance and request intake model and retrain their own staff as well as their business customers. Much of the resistance came from the BI&A staff, who prided themselves on being the "go-to" people for certain business areas.

In addition to their new governance and demand management processes, the team created more formal processes for the delivery of their analyses that allowed them to be more effective business partners (see Figure 4.3). The important lesson learned is that any new process discipline requires training, education, and the ability to adjust as business conditions change.

If the analytic team wants to define boundaries around the scope of their support within the organization, consider establishing an analytic portfolio. The objective of the portfolio is to support discrete business priorities across the company, avoiding siloed solutions. It consolidates different long-term business objectives and actions needing a common

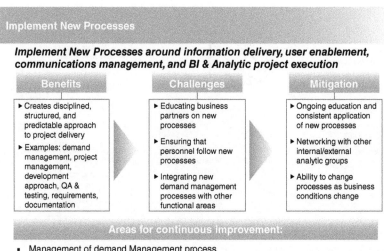

Implement New Processes

Implement New Processes around information delivery, user enablement, communications management, and BI & Analytic project execution

Benefits	Challenges	Mitigation
▶ Creates disciplined, structured, and predictable approach to project delivery ▶ Examples: demand management, project management, development approach, QA & testing, requirements, documentation	▶ Educating business partners on new processes ▶ Ensuring that personnel follow new processes ▶ Integrating new demand management processes with other functional areas	▶ Ongoing education and consistent application of new processes ▶ Networking with other internal/external analytic groups ▶ Ability to change processes as business conditions change

Areas for continuous improvement:

- Management of demand Management process
- Balancing tactical and strategic analytic intelligence delivery
- Be better consultants to business partners

Figure 4.3 BI&A Implement New Processes

set of data or analysis techniques, and helps prioritize investments the team needs to make to achieve specific goals.

Regardless of the size of the analytic team or organization, a reporting mechanism to internal customers assists everyone in understanding and communicating the work that's being done and who it's being done for and determining the work effort's importance to the organization. This will assist the team in finding commonality across requests (which can lead to more strategic self-service information delivery projects) or in uncovering unnecessary information or analytic requests that don't align to business goals.

PROJECT PRIORITIZATION CRITERIA

Organizations use a number of factors in determining whether to move forward with a project, especially if the project requires a hard-dollar investment. Our earlier example shows us that many organizations value their soft-dollar investments as well (but just remember that there's no such thing as a free resource!). Organizations calculate the financial benefits of a project before moving forward, but financial benefits are not the only mechanism for determining whether a project is worth doing. What's different about taking an agile-based approach to prioritization is that you don't have to know everything up front. Agile analytic projects are full of unknowns. Figure 4.4 highlights many of the considerations that organizations make when determining whether to move forward with a project. What makes analytic projects unique is that you often don't know the value of the output upfront: You might find that the results aren't relevant or usable, but you also just might find something that changes your business!

Value-Based Prioritization

Value-based prioritization is one mechanism used to help companies prioritize and select projects by looking at the ways that the project will bring value to the organization or customers. Frequently, a project prioritization matrix is completed to assist the organization with project selection. Selection criteria are created and weighted based on importance.

Value-based prioritization is often seen as part of standard project portfolio management practices. After the project has been classified, project team members complete a high-level assessment of the effort and cost required to implement the project. If the organization doesn't have experience with a particular type of project, they may seek estimates from third party vendors or consultants or just give it their best guess.

Analytic teams benefit a lot from value-based prioritization since with an analysis project, you can never be exactly sure what the output of your project will be. You may not uncover anything useful, but on the other hand, you might find something groundbreaking.

More and more organizations are carving out budgets for innovation projects. Many companies are building out "innovation labs" to jumpstart breakthrough ideas. Analytics are absolutely a part of innovation capabilities, and many companies fund analytic ideas with no more than a leap of faith. Still, you want to ensure that there is a mechanism for validating and prioritizing innovation ideas. Innovation must be aligned to strategic business objectives. Most innovation teams don't take an idea past a prototype; there still needs to be a formal mechanism for taking that prototype and making it operational.

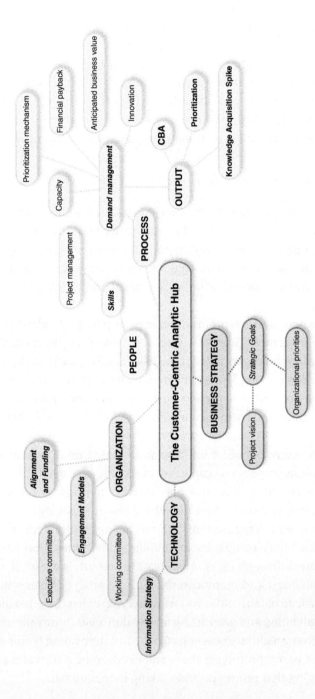

Figure 4.4 Project Justification Considerations

Financial-Based Prioritization

If your analytic project is coupled to a larger strategic initiative and requires investments (resources, data, technology), you may want to take a more traditional financial-based approach to prioritization.

Since there are direct and indirect costs associated with implementing projects, an additional step in the prioritization process is to determine the financial impact. The process of making long-term financial investment decisions is called capital budgeting. Since there may be a significant financial investment through the duration of the project, the project needs to be financially justified. Many organizations have a formal cost-benefit analysis (CBA) process that considers the time value of money. The CBA includes several key metrics that assist the organization in project evaluation and selection. Typical financial metrics include the following:

Payback Period The payback period measures the length of time required to recoup the amount of the initial investment. It is calculated by dividing the initial investment by the estimated annual cash inflows through increased revenues or cost savings/avoidance. Often, during project selection, cash inflows are not known and may need to be estimated. The rule of thumb is that projects with a shorter payback period are preferable. Payback period is typically expressed in years.

Present Value and Net Present Value Present value (PV) calculates the current worth of a future sum of money or cash flow stream given a specified rate of return. Future cash flows are discounted at the discount rate (or minimum required rate of return for an organization). Net present value (NPV) represents the sum of the present values of individual cash flows over a period of time minus the initial investment cost. Each cash inflow or outflow is discounted back to its present value. If NPV is positive, then the organization should consider the investment.

The PV and NPV calculations provide ways to estimate the time value of money. The premise behind the time value of money is that money today has a different value today than in the future. The difference exists due to inflation and the opportunity to earn interest.

Internal Rate of Return The internal rate of return (IRR) represents the rate of growth that the project is anticipated to generate. IRR measures the yield of an investment and is used to compare the expected profitability of a project. IRR is helpful when calculating the project profitability relative to other investment opportunities.

Return on Investment ROI metrics are used to help:
- Investors understand/evaluate the value of their investment and compare it to other investments;
- Define the overall profit of investment as a percentage of the amount invested; and
- Understand if the benefits of project are worth the cost.

The larger the project and the more dependent workstreams there are, the more formal the CBA process generally becomes. For example, if the expected benefits of an analytic project are necessary to fund a large project, the assumptions will be carefully documented and used as inputs into the CBA.

KNOWLEDGE ACQUISITION SPIKES

The challenge with new analytic projects is that there are many unknowns, making it difficult to estimate the duration or effort required to complete a project. The biggest unknown for many organizations centers on the data: If it's not an area that's been tackled before, the data will be in likely disparate systems and of dubious quality.

> ABP's analytic executive steering committee only met formally once a month; they came together for a special session to discuss the retention initiative. The data sciences team outlined their current work-in-progress and recommended some trade-offs and de-prioritization of existing work in order to meet the needs of the new project. The steering committee gives Rebecca permission to lead a two-week data spike.

In an agile project, sometimes you need to allocate time toward knowledge acquisition. In this instance, the steering committee wants to better understand the amount of data work that is involved to determine this project's potential overall impact on other projects. While they acknowledge that the retention project is important, there are several other high-impact analytic projects underway that could be impacted by the reallocation of resources. The data spike is a time-boxed event allowing the team to explore the availability and quality of data needed to answer the business question.

> Rebecca goes back to Sherry with the good news. "We've got approval to do a timeboxed assessment of your data. This step is important in helping the data sciences team better understand your data, where the gaps are, and the amount of effort required to pull it all together for the analysis. Once we complete the assessment, we'll have the information we need to move forward."

SUMMARY

Nothing worthwhile is ever free—and your analytic team shouldn't be, either. Even if you don't have a formal chargeback mechanism in your organization, find a way to value the team's effort so that you can make effective trade-offs in valuing and prioritizing analytic work. Demand management helps teams remove bottlenecks and improve the flow of work, but governance still remains an important mechanism for determining which work should be done. In prioritizing work, organizations use a number of methods, including value-based and innovation projects—where the financial value of the outcome cannot be quantified, but the organization believes the project is the right thing to do; and more formal financial-based prioritization methods, such as a CBA. Since there are so many unknowns in analytic projects, consider a knowledge acquisition spike to uncover more information before moving forward.

CHAPTER 5

Analytics—the Agile Way

A nalytic teams have a lot of different project delivery methods to choose from, each with their own pros and cons. If the analytic team is using a delivery methodology, most often it's the standard waterfall delivery model, where work falls in a phased, sequential approach. However, due to the ambiguous nature of analytic projects, agile methods provide analytic teams with much-needed structure and delivery discipline, while respecting the creative and iterative nature of analytic projects. Navigating the agile family of methodologies can be confusing for any team. This section provides a brief overview of the most prevalent methods and recommendation for selecting the right method for your team (see Figure 5.1).

GETTING STARTED

Isabel sits down with her stakeholders. "Okay, folks, let me tell you a little about how my team works and how we'd like to engage with you as we go through this project. We know that the quality of our deliverable is critical, but we're also sensitive about speed. Analytics projects are unique, since we don't often know what the outcome will be. But we don't want to go hide out for six months without giving you any insights along the way.

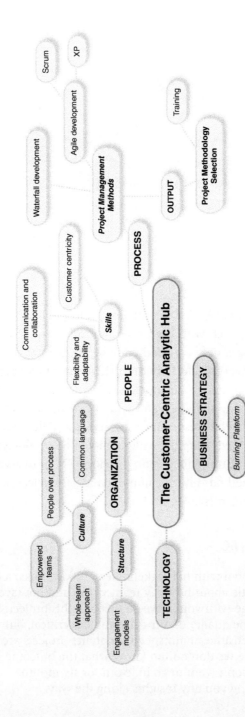

Figure 5.1 Analytic Project Management Decision Considerations

"Back when I started at the company, we didn't use any project management methodologies to run our projects, and it was chaotic! Nobody knew what anyone was working on and everyone had different ideas about how the work should be done. We even got into trouble because we found that one of our analysts had personally identifiable information on his laptop. We didn't have any way to understand if our work was really important to the business and there wasn't any mechanism for prioritizing projects.

"Management got really tired of that. They hired a new executive to run the team and put some control mechanisms in place. The problem was that we went in the opposite direction: We'd gone from a free-for-all to a bureaucracy overnight. The new process included nine different approval stage-gates. We weren't allowed to move to the next phase of work unless everything was perfect—and nothing in analytics is perfect the first time! Nobody in the business wanted to leverage our team because it took too long to get approvals and to complete the work. The business started hiring consultants to do the work that we were supposed to do! They said we weren't customer-friendly and couldn't deliver in their time frames.

"As you can imagine, that executive didn't last very long. I was promoted to lead the team, and as part of my new responsibility did some research on some of the newer project delivery methods that have gained a lot of traction in the IT space. We needed to find something that respected the creative and iterative aspects of analytic delivery, but gave us some structure and discipline. I found that many companies were starting to use something called agile. But the more I looked into it, the more confusing it got—there were a lot of different agile methodologies to choose from—how would I know which one would be right for us?"

UNDERSTANDING WATERFALL

The statistician, Dr. Edward Deming, began working with auto manufacturers in the 1950s to create continuous improvement and quality cycles, popularly known as the Plan-Do-Check-Act (PDCA) model (also referred to as the Deming Cycle or Circle). Over time, the strict approach to process quality in manufacturing was adapted to the software development processes in the form of the software development lifecycle (SDLC). The SDLC is one of the original "waterfall" processes and follows a highly structured sequence of events from analysis and design, development, testing, and release. The SDLC provides the underpinnings of the traditional software development model, most popularly used in methodologies such as the Project Management Institute's project management methodology.

The waterfall model follows a phased, sequential approach, as shown in Figure 5.2.

The analytic development lifecycle (ADLC) follows a similar waterfall approach, as shown in Figure 5.3.

The primary criticism of the waterfall methods is that they attempt to be predictive. All of the requirements are gathered upfront, the design completed, a project plan created, and then the team runs off to build whatever the customer initially asked for. Changes to project scope are managed through sometimes-inflexible change control processes. The challenge is that that development cycle can take a long time; often when the final product is delivered, it may not be what the customer wanted or expected.

More often than not, analytic teams aren't using any project methodology at all in their projects. While that may make a lot of

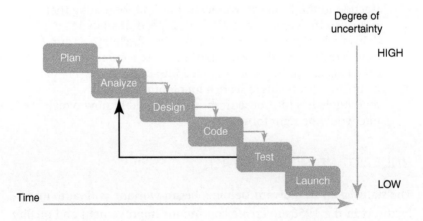

Figure 5.2 Waterfall Development Process

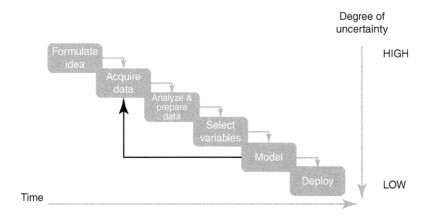

Figure 5.3 Waterfall Analytic Development Process

sense for smaller "just-do-it" work, lack of a disciplined approach can result in chaos once a model reaches the business and technology deployment phase. The beauty of agile methodologies is that they are adaptable and flexible in nature—they provide a level of control without being heavy-handed or introducing a lot of process overhead.

THE HEART OF AGILE

In 1986, Hirotaka Takeuchi and Ikujiro Nonaka published an article in the *Harvard Business Review* titled the "The New New Product Development Game" (Takeuchi & Nonaka, 1986). They argued that in product development cycles, organizations could no longer solely compete on quality, cost, and product differentiation: Speed and flexibility were equally critical elements of the development process. The sequential development process used by many companies did not support business agility. The authors recommended that a "rugby" approach be used instead, "where a team tries to go the distance as a unit, passing the ball back and forth—[to] better serve today's competitive requirements." Instead of a sequential approach that hands work off across functional areas, the rugby approach uses an integrated multidisciplinary team working together from start to finish.

By moving from a linear to an integrated approach, experimentation is encouraged. The close interaction between diverse team members stimulates ideas and discussions, acting as a catalyst for innovative product development.

Encouraged by Takeuchi and Nonaka's research, in the early 1990s, the software development community began to evaluate the rugby approach as a method to replace waterfall methods in project development cycles. There was growing recognition that the SDLC was not always effective at delivering value within complex development projects. In a waterfall project, all scope, time, and costs are defined at the start of the project when uncertainty is high. For complex projects, where the domain might not be well understood, the sequential nature doesn't allow for frequent feedback loops. Often, when the project was "complete" it was delivered late, over budget, and not meeting user needs.

Frustrated with poor alignment between waterfall and complex technology projects, a number of practitioners independently set out to create more effective ways to deliver products and services to customers and end users. While the methodologies varied widely, the approaches increased the development team's ability to (as agile is defined) "move quickly and easily" and unshackle itself from the process- and documentation-centric SDLC or ADLC model. These methods manifested into a number of different agile methodologies. The most popular of the methodologies, Scrum, honors the spirit of Takeuchi and Nonaka's recommendations on using the rugby metaphor to increase business agility.

THE AGILE MANIFESTO/DECLARATION OF INTERDEPENDENCE

In 2001, several leading practitioners and proponents of these agile software development methodologies convened at a resort in Utah. The group shared best practices, identified common themes, and ulti-mately outlined a common purpose for agile practitioners. This purpose statement became The Agile Manifesto and established the grounding principles behind the agile philosophy for software development.

While the primary users of agile are software developers, the prin-ciples and techniques apply to other project environments. Practition-ers can apply any of the agile principles to their own projects to drive customer value, productivity, and efficiency. In fact, agile is often considered more of a philosophy than a methodology. Simply put, the practitioners stated:

❝ We are uncovering better ways of developing software
by doing it and helping others do it.

Through this work we have come to value:

Individuals and interactions		Processes and tools
Working software	OVER	Comprehensive documentation
Customer collaboration		Contract negotiation
Responding to change		Following a plan

That is, while there is value in the items on the right, ❞
we value the items on the left more.

(2001, Beck, K., Beedle, M., Bennekum, A., Cockburn, A., Cunningham, W. et al.)

You've probably noticed that the Manifesto is kept at a very high level. An important point is that agile focuses on the big picture, and while the values are uniform across the frameworks, the details that encompass each agile methodology will be implemented differently.

Let's briefly take a look at each value pair, as shown in Table 5.1.

Scrum and Scrum variants are by far the most popularly utilized methodologies. Interestingly, not only are a large percentage of companies adapting the methodologies to fit into their organizations, but we're also seeing an increase in hybrid methodologies that leverage right-sized practices from several of these methods. The implication for analytic teams is that most of these methodologies don't work well for you in isolation—there's no one-size-fits-all. Don't fall for the "my way or the highway" mantra positioned by a lot of external influencers. The following section will provide an overview of several popular methodologies, and then we'll focus creating your own agile analytic framework.

The good news is that the core tenets of agile are at the heart of each of these methodologies. How you select a methodology depends on your organization, your culture, and the type of project that you're working on. If you're new to agile, Scrum may be a good place to start

Table 5.1 Agile Analytic Values

Agile Values	What It Means	Implication for Analytics
Individuals and interactions over processes and tools	This principle highlights the value of people as the foundation of the project. Processes and tools are important, but it is people that get the work done. Agile emphasizes teamwork and collaboration.	Analytic groups need to integrate with the whole team—business stakeholders, application developers, ETL developers, etc. throughout the analytic development process—and work together.
Working software over comprehensive documentation	Agile's focus on delivering customer value places an emphasis on getting working software into customer hands quickly. This is not to say that documentation is not important, but that documentation needs to add value.	Focus on working together and creating a common language instead of trying to fix a broken development cycle with process overhead, templates, and documentation. Uncover what information is important to capture and institutionalize.
Customer collaboration over contract negotiation	A primary difference between traditional waterfall methods and agile is that the customer is a key resource that is often embedded with the delivery team. Your customers are best positioned to tell you what they want or need through the project lifecycle, not just in an upfront contract negotiation.	Business stakeholders and domain specialists are critical throughout the analytic lifecycle. They are best positioned to define what's important to the business and how the business works. Establishing relationships and building trust are important elements of deploying effective, relevant analytics into business processes.
Responding to change over following a plan	Agile's original intent was to facilitate better delivery of working, relevant software to end users. Anyone who has worked on a software project knows how quickly requirements or business needs change. The ability to adapt to customer needs is a critical point of difference in agile.	A key difference in an analytic project is that you don't always know what you will find. Analytic projects are iterative by nature, requiring constant revalidation of the business problem, the data sources used to analyze the problem, and the outcome.

as it provides a simple framework that can expand and scale as your team gains confidence and maturity.

The bad news is that there's a lot of confusion out in the marketplace. Many consultants have created sub-methodologies and frameworks, each with their distinct characteristics, ceremonies, and practices. Unlike more mature methodologies, there's no single body of knowledge to use as a guidepost. So teams must carefully select the agile frameworks and practices that will work best in the context of their organization.

SELECTING THE RIGHT METHODOLOGY

It's important to note that agile methodologies are not appropriate for all types of projects and organizations, and that using an agile methodology is not a guarantee of project success. Agile analytic projects work best in environments where complex decision making requires an iterative development approach. Political and cultural challenges may necessitate a plan-driven approach, as will an environment that is too far over the edge of chaos and requires structure. Even if your project seems well suited to an agile methodology, cultural or organizational barriers may inhibit the success of the methodology. After all, agile projects are all about team empowerment—that in and of itself requires a significant cultural shift within many organizations.

> In our ABP project, Isabel says: "As we work with our customers, we're flexible on the methodology that we use. One of the things that we uncovered early on is that different projects require different approaches. In fact, as we learned more about each of the methodologies, we found elements that we could pull together and make our own. Even more importantly, our internal customers are using different delivery methodologies in their projects— most of our work needs to integrate in some way with theirs. Agile gives us the flexibility we need to link our work together.
>
> "When we created the methodology that our team would use, we first looked at Scrum since it seemed to be the most prevalent method."

Scrum

Jeff Sutherland and Ken Schwaber, the founders of Scrum, derived the methodology from Takeuchi and Nonaka's work, applying the rugby metaphor to software development practices. With its lightweight project delivery approach and applicability to different types of projects, Scrum has rapidly become one of the most widely used agile project management methods. Scrum leverages a simple iterative framework that is appealing to organizations looking to incorporate agile into their development processes. The broad appeal of Scrum is enhanced by its applicability to multiple types of projects beyond the software development realm.

Scrum structures work into cycles called "sprints" of typically no more than 30 days in duration. During a sprint, the development team selects customer requirements in the form of user stories from a prioritized list. This allows the team to work on functionality that will deliver the most value to the customer. The goal at the end of each sprint is to have a potentially shippable product delivered to end users for feedback. Sprints are rolled into a predetermined release schedule.

Scrum features several distinct roles:

The *product owner* facilitates the process of identifying and prioritizing customer requirements and serves as the liaison between the development team and the end users. Requirements are captured as user stories and are organized and prioritized in a product backlog. At the start of each sprint, the project team selects the highest priority stories, estimates the work effort, and then plans the sprint based on the amount of work the team believes they can accomplish during the sprint. Once the sprint is complete, the product backlog is groomed and reprioritized by the product owner, and the team again selects the next highest priority requirements.

The *ScrumMaster* is responsible for facilitating (not directing!) project activities. His/her focus area is on keeping the team aligned to the Scrum process and removing impediments or interference with the team's progress. ScrumMasters may have a technical background, which helps smooth communication between the development team and the business community.

The *development team* is a cross-functional representation of people performing the work. The rule of thumb is to have five to nine people on the team. The development team members may have a variety of roles, such as programmers, architects, testers, database administrators, and so on. Scrum empowers the development team to self-organize. This means that the team determines how the work will be performed.

> "The simplicity of Scrum was really appealing," says Isabel. "Basically, we have three roles on the team. We ask our business sponsors to take the role of the product owner. We have a dedicated project coordinator role for our ScrumMaster—we make sure that they're trained in both traditional waterfall and Scrum methodologies, depending on the type of project that we're on. If the project is large enough, we'll ask architects, data modelers, ETL specialists, and data scientists to form the development team. Once we get the green light to get moving on this project, we'll determine who should participate and then get a meeting together."

eXtreme Programming (XP)

XP is a software development methodology based on four core values: simplicity, communication, feedback, and courage. XP's strength is rapid analysis, design, coding, and testing cycles within short iterations, typically one week in duration with a collocated team. The emphasis on face-to-face collaboration eliminates the need for the team to run through long requirements for design and testing phases. Similar to Scrum, the team selects several user stories in each iteration and completes all development phases for each story. The software is deployed on a predetermined basis (often weekly) for review and feedback. A differentiator for XP is the technical discipline and sophistication of testing practices, which are highly automated.

XP is not widely used as a stand-alone agile methodology. Most teams incorporate XP technical practices into their processes as a way of ensuring quality in their deliverables.

> Isabel walks back to her office with the new junior analyst on the data sciences team, Jeremy.

"I think you're really going to like working on this project, Jeremy. It will be a good opportunity for you to learn some of our team's operating principals. As we got deeper into Scrum, we realized that something was missing," Isabel sits down and leans back in her chair. "Scrum provides a rhythm—it's like the beat of the drum—but it doesn't prescribe practices for getting the work done. Everything we do in analytics is pretty unique, but there are a lot of things that we wanted to make repeatable. We came to the realization that we needed to create our own technical best practices and bring them into the Scrum framework.

"I was talking with some friends of mine in the IT department. The told me about an agile methodology called eXtreme Programming, or XP. Their group had been able to incorporate some of the XP technical practices recommended into their Scrum implementation."

Isabel goes on, "XP has twelve supporting practices and several of them were particularly important to us. We liked the XP concepts of Simple Design, Pair Programming, Refactoring, Collective Code Ownership, and Coding Standards. We took these concepts and made them relevant to our team's work. While these aspects of our agile analytic methodology might not be interesting to the broader organization, everyone appreciates the outcome in the quality of our work and our ability to consistently deliver regardless of the project. Once you get into this project, we'll assign a mentor to work with you and teach you some of the XP practices in our day-to-day work. Remember that agile is all about continuous improvement and providing customer value, so if you see ways that we can be doing our job better, don't be afraid to speak up.

"And finally, we use lean as a management philosophy and apply it to all of our other tools, techniques, and processes. Lean teaches us to see everything from the customer's perspective, only doing work that will add value to them. This helps us avoid process for process's sake." (See Figure 5.4.)

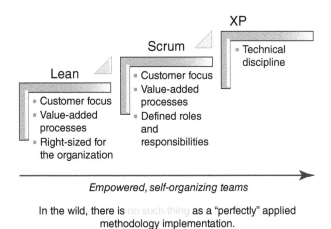

Empowered, self-organizing teams

In the wild, there is no such thing as a "perfectly" applied
methodology implementation.

Figure 5.4 The Team's Agile Framework

SUMMARY

Analytic teams have many different options when selecting a delivery
methodology. There is no "one size fits all" model. Cultural factors play
an important role when selecting your methodology; it's important to
understand specific needs and constraints within your organization.
With its simple framework, Scrum provides a good starting point as
it's easily extensible. Technical practices within XP can be incorporated
to provide the team with more technical discipline in their delivery
approach. Regardless of which method you select, follow the guiding principles of The Agile Manifesto: Focus on customer value and
high-quality deliverables.

CHAPTER 6

Analytic Planning Hierarchies

A gile development leverages planning approaches at series of different levels. At the highest level sits business strategy definition and planning, a concept we briefly touched on in Chapter 3, Getting Your Analytic Project off the Ground and Chapter 4, Project Justification and Prioritization. However, it's important to recognize that these lower-level project-planning activities also fit into broader organizational strategies. Bringing these different planning hierarchies together is critical in setting organizational priorities, aligning resources, and agreeing on and evaluating results. No analytic project is an island—the analytic initiative aligns to strategic business objectives at the highest level, but also to other shorter-term goals. As you're planning your analytic release, outline the expected outputs from our projects and set release dates (see Figure 6.1).

ANALYTIC PROJECT EXAMPLE

As we think about release planning for our customer retention project, we have to anticipate the type of work that we will be performing. Again, we're not trying to be completely predictive or plan our project to death, but we do need to understand and define discrete

Figure 6.1 Analytic Planning Considerations

deliverables. Coming out of the data spike, the team roughs out the work that will need to be accomplished so that it can be presented to the executive committee. Once the team has an idea of how much work is contained in the overall project, it can estimate some release dates.

People often believe that detailed requirements are inappropriate in an agile project. However, even in Scrum, teams can write detailed requirements if the team finds them useful (written detail generally is useful when sharing information across a distributed team). If the team is unsure of where to start, begin with the user story format and add more detail as needed. The "inspect and adapt" cycle in the retrospective will provide an opportunity for the team to provide that feedback. The team should not use documentation as an excuse to not have face-to-face sessions.

Analytic teams generally produce three types of output: informational, directional, and operational analytics. A large analytic initiative will likely have deliverables that encompass all three areas.

Informational In an informational project, the team is evaluating and analyzing data to answer a business question. The goal of a project like this may be to gain more information, but the results may not be used in any directional or production capacity. The output of this information may or may not be used to influence other business decisions. Organizations widely use informational projects to prove out a particular capability or gauge feasibility of executing on a larger scale project (i.e., proof-of-concept). Most informational projects are throwaway.

Directional Directional projects provide insight that is used to influence business decisions. While the model or score might not be used in any operational system or capacity, analytic results lead to changes in business processes. For example, one company discovered some distinctive web usage patterns in certain customers that influenced their at-risk score. The directional analysis triggered some design changes in the company's website.

Operational In an operational analytic project, the goal is to create some predictive algorithm or score to deploy in an operational environment. In our hypothetical project, we're going to take the customer risk scores and make them available in the CRM system. The algorithm might also be deployed in a real-time scoring capability. For example, when a customer logs into their account online, a scoring mechanism is triggered. Customers may receive dynamically generated special offers depending on their risk propensity score.

Isabel's team anticipates that the next step of project is to analyze the customer data, model the data to identify both descriptive and predictive customer segments that can be utilized within the retention strategy, as well as assist in the implementation of the new segments into that strategy. The team's output will include a mix of informational, directional, and operational analytics that the business will consider for a variety of treatments yet to be determined.

Prior to beginning the segmentation analyses, the team covers six areas to determine the output of the customer retention segmentation and model development work, specifically:

- Identifying customer attributes to use in the segmentation
- Identifying customer populations to study (i.e., all customers versus customer segments)
- Defining the types of segmentation that will be used (i.e., business rules, quantiles, supervised and unsupervised clustering)
- Performing segmentation analysis
- Defining the types of output needed to enable the operational strategies (models, scores, attributes, etc.)
- Providing the variables driving customer churn

INPUTS INTO PLANNING CYCLES

The analytic Scrum team is accountable for sprint and daily planning. However, an understanding of portfolio, product, and release planning is helpful in understanding the role the team plays in larger strategic planning activities (see Figure 6.2).

To illustrate the concept of multilevel planning, we can take a look at our retention project:

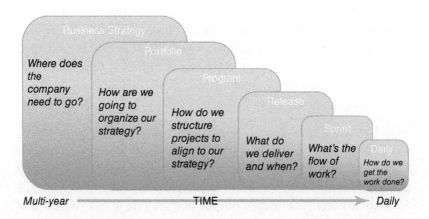

Figure 6.2 Planning Horizon

Business Strategy Planning At the business strategy level, our company has a strategic initiative around improving customer experience. Initiatives that fall into this category are multiyear in scope and are organization-wide.

Portfolio Planning At a portfolio level, there may be many programs and projects within the organization aligned to customer experience. For example, in our retention project, there may be initiatives tied to product development, operational system modernization projects, pricing, and so on, that all roll up to the "customer experience" umbrella. In our case, there's a portfolio for the CRM implementation, which has many projects associated with it. Portfolio planning or management helps the organization determine the projects that should be worked on, their priority and funding. A portfolio typically encompasses a group of projects. Many organizations and IT departments organize their business models around their portfolios.

The portfolio planning activities do not typically involve the analytic Scrum team. However, the input of senior architects and/or technical leads is an important component of the planning for larger analytic projects, or analytic output that might end up embedded in an operational system. Enterprise technical constraints, considerations, and standards are factored into the decision-making process. IT platform development decisions can also carry through into the individual portfolio planning process.

Program Planning At the program level, we coordinate the work effort of multiple projects aligned to a single business objective. Program management helps organizations manage schedule, cost/benefits, and effort across multiple project workstreams. Program management facilitates the integration points and dependencies between different projects. Our analytic project may roll up into a larger program (as a component of a larger system development project), or it may be its own stand-alone project. What changes in those instances is how the organization engages and aligns releases, but not necessarily how the work is accomplished at the sprint level.

Is it okay if we use agile and the rest of our organization uses a traditional waterfall methodology? Absolutely. Program deliverables can be coordinated at the release level. How the individual teams perform the work is generally less important than aligning the delivery dates of the output. Regardless, the teams should sit down and discuss the expected dependencies between their projects and identify how the integration points will be coordinated.

Release Planning At the release level, we're aligning the delivery of those analytics with integration points across the larger CRM portfolio. While the output of each sprint is designed to be "shippable" (i.e., usable by the customer), most organizations deliver their work on a release cycle. Each release may encompass several sprints. Some organizations use a practice called continuous deployment (or delivery) where features are released to customers as they are completed. However, for in an IT development, the release schedule may be much more formal. The concept of a release is largely an IT construct, but it does have implications for analytic teams who are integrating their work into larger development projects. For example, an insurance company might be implementing a new claims administration system. It delivers functionality to the claims organization in incremental releases on a predefined schedule. If the analytic team is developing a claims fraud detection model and there is a dependency on some functionality in the administration system, the delivery of those two components would be aligned at the release level. Many IT organizations use a biannual release schedule for major application version releases, but put out enhancements on a quarterly release schedule.

Release planning is not a once-and-done activity, but takes place during each sprint. The initial release planning activity follows product envisioning. If the product is new, the initial release plans may not be complete or precise. As the organization learns more as development work is completed, the release plan will be updated during the sprint reviews. The extended Scrum team (stakeholders, developers) participates in the release planning process so it will be able to balance the technical and business trade-offs.

Release planning process inputs include outputs from product planning: product vision documents, high-level product backlog, and product roadmap. If the development team's velocity is known it is helpful in determining what work might be achievable within the product's cost or time constraints. If velocity is unknown, then the team can forecast.

Sprint Planning At the sprint level, the Scrum team selects high-priority backlog items and decomposes the items into tasks during the planning process. The tasks form the basis of the sprint backlog. This level of planning is the primary focus for our analytic team's retention project. Detailed sprint planning will be covered in a later chapter.

Daily Planning The most detailed level of planning occurs at the daily level during the daily Scrum meeting. During this meeting, each team member outlines (1) what he or she has worked on since the last daily meeting, (2) what is planned for today, and (3) any impediments that the team member has in completing that work.

To summarize, product development uses a multilevel planning approach starting with business strategy and ending with execution at the daily Scrum level. As the business defines their strategy, a portfolio of development initiatives emerges. At the portfolio planning level, the organization may group like projects or products under a portfolio: In fact, many companies structure their organizations around portfolios. Product planning activities generate a list of user requirements captured as the product backlog. The prioritized high-level product backlog is organized into a series of planned releases, often in the form of a product roadmap. Each release may encompass several sprints. The analytic Scrum team selects detailed product backlog items during sprint planning and decomposes them into tasks. Daily planning occurs in the form of the daily Scrum, where development team members discuss progress and impediments.

RELEASE PLANNING

In a release, analytic delivery teams formally deliver their results to their customers. Recall that in a sprint, the work is reviewed with customers and is complete in accordance with the team's definition of done, but most likely isn't ready to be deployed in a business environment. In a release, the team provides complete functionality in some form (in our analytic project it could be a completed predictive model, scored data, or segments). In a software development cycle, releases may occur every three to six months and encompass many sprints. Release plans provide fixed dates when the output of the project is released to end customers.

Releases are important in helping the organization understand what the analytic team is developing and delivering and when. While this is important to setting customer expectations, it's also an important organizational planning tool for creating a predictable delivery rhythm. Release planning also helps the analytic Scrum team to align the work toward a series of set goals.

The team's release plan has four separate alignments: Data development and exploration, model and segmentation development, model hardening and business implementation planning, and operational model deployment. Each release provides an additional go-forward decision point for the organization while individual sprints create momentum in the work and allows the organization to incrementally change course. The release dates keep the team focused on larger milestones and help prevent perfectionism. Without a defined release date, many teams fall into the trap of Parkinson's law—that is, teams will work within the time that they are allowed. Theoretically, without end dates, the team will continue to analyze and tweak data and models into infinity.

The release planning process happens early on in the project lifecycle. But like all things in agile, the release planning is not a once-and-done activity. In fact, many teams evaluate their release plan at the end of each sprint.

ANALYTIC RELEASE PLAN

The timebox enforced by the release dates keeps teams working on the principle of "good enough." If the team believes that incremental improvements can be made to the final deliverable, that's a discussion that team members can have with the product owner. If the product owner believes that additional work will add value, then additional sprints can be used for that work.

Unlike our sprint review, which focuses on work completed during our one-week sprints, our release showcases the overall functionality and completeness of our results. Goals are assigned to each release, and the sprints within that release cycle focus on achieving that goal. What functionality goes into a release is negotiable. Release goals (but not dates!) may be altered if the team can't complete the desired work product in time.

Our example analytic release plan in Table 6.1 outlines our releases. On the left hand side, there are five different release themes. Release themes detail what will be delivered, not how. In your own projects, you may identify many other areas that will be important to you. An individual release can have functionality tied to different themes. As the project moves forward, additional releases and release themes can be defined as appropriate.

Release Train

If our analytic work is tied to a larger business portfolio or program initiative, we may need our deliverables to align to specific release dates set by those projects.

At the program level, release trains can be used as an approach to align vision, planning, and team interdependency. The release train provides cross-team synchronization to facilitate fast flow at the program level. A published schedule of capabilities is issued, and all development teams need to have their work completed at the appointed time.

At the release train level, an enterprise product backlog exists with three additional levels of backlog: portfolio, program, and team. Each team performs its own sprint with work from their feature-area backlog and coordinates across teams using an integration approach known as the Scrum of Scrums.

A Scrum of Scrums (SoS) is a periodic standup meeting that includes representatives from each Scrum team. The goal is to coordinate work across the teams. Delegates may include the team's

Table 6.1 Analytic Release Plan

Release #	Release 1	Release 2	Release 3	Release 4
Release Theme	*Data development and exploration*	*Segmentation and model development*	*Model hardening and business implementation planning*	*Operational model deployment*
Data development and exploration	Acquiring and preparing the needed data for the segmentation and modeling	Exploration of additional data sources		
Model and segmentation development		Development of segments and predictive models		
Model and segmentation rollout			Completion of segments and predictive models	
Business deployment strategy			Identification of areas where models and segments will be used to influence business decisions Determining organizational change management strategy	Creation of persona-based segments Launch of marketing campaigns for high-risk customers / user segments Integration of customer risk score in CRM application
Operational deployment			Determining operational deployment strategy	Productionalize model development ETL

ScrumMaster and an analyst-developer who can best speak to the interdependencies of the work. The Scrum of Scrums may also have its own ScrumMaster. SoS meetings do not occur daily—the teams determine the appropriate frequency. Similar to the teams' daily standup meetings, the SoS provides a roundtable for the following questions:

- What has my team done since we last met that could affect the other teams?
- What will my team do before we meet again that could affect other teams?
- What problems is my team having that it could use help from the other teams to resolve?

Since the SoS does not meet daily, consider a fourth question: Is my team about to do something that could get in another team's way? By providing the larger team with advance notice that something has changed (or will change), the group can plan more appropriately.

SUMMARY

No analytic project is an island! Organizations plan at multiple levels: At the highest level sits business strategy: big picture multiyear objectives. Those business strategies are decomposed into smaller components that the organization delivers on. Depending on the scope of the strategy, organizations structure different portfolios and programs to coordinate the work effort of smaller projects. Your analytic project may align to a portfolio/program or be a stand-alone project. Regardless, defining release dates for the project helps keep it on track and provides accountability to the broader organization.

CHAPTER 7

Our Analytic Scrum Framework

he analytic team uses Scrum as the primary methodology for managing the flow of work throughout their large analytic projects. Scrum work is organized into fixed-duration iterations or cycles called sprints. Within a sprint, there are several key milestone activities related to planning, execution, reviews, and retrospectives. This section provides an overview of each phase within our Scrum framework (see Figure 7.1).

GETTING STARTED

The analytic team receives good news. Rebecca meets with the team. "The customer retention project was approved by the steering committee. We have permission to go forward with the project. Since this is a high priority, we're going to assign two modelers from our team, an ETL developer, and a couple of dedicated business data subject matter experts full-time to the project. Since the output of this project may result in changes to our customer relationship management application, I'm going to

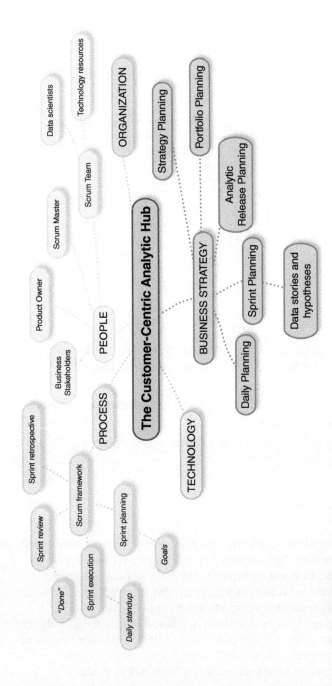

Figure 7.1 Analytic Scrum Framework Considerations

coordinate with IT for additional support and guidance. We'll include them in our kickoff meeting so that they're aware of the work that the team will be doing."

At the kickoff meeting, Rebecca looks around the room. "I see we have a bunch of new faces on our project. Great! The purpose of getting together today is to give you an overview of the Scrum framework and how we use it in our analytic projects. For those of you in IT who might be using Scrum, we do it a little differently here to account for some of the unique needs we have in analytic projects—so I'll give you an overview of the traditional methodology that you might be familiar with and then how we've adapted it."

THE SCRUM FRAMEWORK

In Scrum, development work is performed in cycles known as *sprints*. Another term for sprint is *iteration,* and while 30 days is the rule of thumb for most IT development teams, iteration cycles can be different durations in time (e.g., XP tends to use a shorter one- to two-week cycle). The Scrum team and product owner determine the length of the sprint, which should stay consistent through the duration of the project, and the number of sprints within a release cycle. Keeping a sprint between one to four weeks in duration makes it easier to incrementally plan, execute, and receive feedback. ADP uses one-week sprints in their analytic projects as a way to continually showcase results.

Like most agile activities, sprints are timeboxed with a defined start and end date. The purpose of timeboxing a sprint—keeping it to a fixed duration—is to organize the work and help the team manage scope. The timebox helps the team to establish a limit to their work in progress, forces prioritization of work, avoids overanalysis, and demonstrates ongoing progress to customers.

The goal at the end of each sprint is to demonstrate working functionality to customers as a measure of progress and to capture feedback. A new sprint directly follows a completed sprint unless the product is complete or there is no additional funding available. A project typically encompasses multiple sprints, and sprints align to releases, where functionality is delivered to the customer (see Figure 7.2).

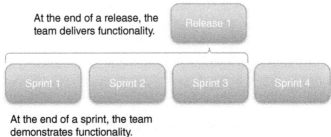

At the end of a release, the team delivers functionality.

At the end of a sprint, the team demonstrates functionality.

Figure 7.2 Sprints Aligned to Releases

Additionally, sprint durations should be consistent throughout the duration of the project unless there is a special situation that the team needs to address (holidays, release dates, retrospective feedback, etc.). If the team cannot meet its commitments to the product backlog (the list of requirements that it is working on) during a sprint, the amount of work the team selected should be altered, not the timeframe of the sprint.

Prior to sprint execution, the team goes through a sprint planning cycle.

> Rebecca continues, "Since the output of an analytic project can be ambiguous—that is, the output is used to influence other user stories for the business—we define it a little differently up front. We run our work in phases for data exploration, data integration, and model development. Within each phase, we will have multiple sprints. The phases aren't mutually exclusive—as an example, sometimes we can move forward into the next phase of development without all of the data sources. But the framework is designed to be flexible enough that we can integrate new data in any phase. Since we want to get feedback quickly, we run in one-week sprints."

SPRINT PLANNING

Since the items in the product backlog likely represent a significant duration of work—more than can be completed in a single sprint—the product owner, development team, and ScrumMaster perform sprint planning at the beginning of each sprint.

In the sprint planning session, the team agrees on a sprint goal to determine what the sprint will achieve. With the goal in mind, the team reviews the highest-priority backlog items (prioritized by the product owner; often represented as user stories) that it believes can be accomplished during the sprint. Remember that a goal of Scrum is to ensure that the team works at a sustainable pace. This pace should reflect the team's normal working capabilities across an extended time period—not 80-hour work weeks!

Think of the sprint goal as a vision statement for the sprint. The sprint goal defines the business purpose and the value of the sprint (see Figure 7.3). The purpose behind defining a shared sprint goal is to align the team during sprint execution. The goal also helps determine which stories should be worked on by the team. Once the sprint goal has been established and sprint execution begins, no changes are permitted that affect that goal, although the goal itself might be redefined.

> "When we define a sprint goal," says Rebecca, "we'll look at the high-priority items on our backlog. For an analytic team, we're always starting with data sources. So our sprint goal in Sprint 1 might be to Identify and Assess Source Data Quality. As the team starts the estimation process, it might limit that sprint goal to just a few high-priority data sources. In our retention project, we know that the customer data tables will be the most important, so our first goal might be specific to that. If the team knows that data source very well and knows that it will go quickly, it might take on some additional work. It's up to the team to decide how much work it can reasonably accomplish in a sprint."

In determining whether the team has the capacity to complete the desired product backlog items within the sprint, the team breaks down the user stories into a set of tasks. This collection of stories and tasks becomes the sprint backlog. The analytic team then estimates the work effort required to complete each task. As a rule of thumb, tasks typically represent no more than eight hours of work effort. When decomposed to this level, the team should have a good sense of the overall work effort and its ability to fit within the sprint.

As a rule of thumb, the sprint planning session is also timeboxed. Since the analytic team runs in one-week sprints, limit the planning session to one to two hours. Spend the first hour selecting product backlog items, and the second hour in preparing the sprint backlog. At the end of the session, the team has completed its sprint backlog, which includes tasks, task estimates, and work assignments. At this stage, the task list for the sprint might not be fully fleshed out, but contains enough detail for the team to begin development work. As the sprint progresses additional tasks can be added. If the team finds that it has extra capacity within the sprint to take on more work, it can coordinate with the product owner to select additional product backlog items.

SPRINT EXECUTION

Once sprint planning is complete, the team gets to work. As a self-organizing unit, the team defines how the task-level work will be done and in what order to best accomplish the sprint goal.

> Isabel says: "A typical sprint cycle in IT is around 30 days; remember, ours is only a week. We found through trial and error that this timeframe provided enough time for our team to complete their work, and also kept the team from overproducing—doing too much analysis or overworking the code. Our customers like the short cycle since we're always funneling information to them. It helps them stay interested and engaged throughout the project. They love being involved in the decision-making process, and at the end of the day it's helped with the business adoption of our results."

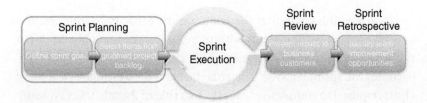

Figure 7.3 Sprint Planning within a Sprint Cycle

Rebecca's team uses the following guidelines during the sprint execution:

- The team is free to ask other people throughout the organization for advice, help, and support during the sprint, but it's not appropriate for others to tell the team what to do, or how to do it.

- Once work begins on a sprint, the backlog items in that sprint cannot be changed (although if the team has extra capacity, it can take on additional work from the product backlog).

- If something occurs during the sprint that impedes work (e.g., data not available or usable; technology platform not ready), the ScrumMaster can end the sprint and restart planning.

- If the team takes on too much work and cannot meet its commitment to the sprint, the product owner can be consulted, possibly resulting in a shift in sprint goals or reorganization of the backlog.

- Team members must meet their commitments to attend daily Scrum meetings and adhere to team practices. Team members are responsible for keeping the sprint backlog up-to-date and visible to team members.

"The key is holding everyone accountable," says Rebecca. "We all have a role to play on these projects—our product owner/sponsor, customers, the team members, and the ScrumMaster. Our goal is to provide an environment that lets the team meet its commitments to the customer. Our customer is accountable for providing guidance and feedback throughout the project."

Source: Schwaber (2009)

DAILY STANDUP

At the start of each day, the Scrum team holds a daily Scrum meeting called the *daily standup* as part of the inspect-and-adapt activities within Scrum. The daily standup meeting is no more than 15 minutes in length and the team members give a round-robin status update by answering the following questions:

- What did I accomplish since the last daily Scrum?
- What do I plan to work on by the next daily Scrum?
- What are the obstacles or impediments that are preventing me from making progress?

The purpose of asking these questions is to ensure that team members are focused on the work at hand, they are progressing toward the sprint goal, and they are addressing any issues that need to be addressed. Don't use your daily standups for problem solving; while issues are brought up, discussions for solving those issues take place after the meeting. This keeps the standup short and focused—remember that the point is to let others know what you've accomplished and what you'll be working on.

> "We hold our daily standup every morning at 8:30 a.m. We found that starting the day when everyone was fresh worked better. Attendance is required. If you can't attend, make sure that someone else on the team can report out on your behalf. We do have a teleconference line set up for the call for remote attendees, but if you're in the building, we want you here. We start our meetings promptly—we keep a penalty jar in our war room. If you're late, then we fine you $1 and the money goes to charity. We made a lot of money the first few months we started implementing Scrum!" Rebecca laughs. "In each meeting, we only ask that you answer the three questions—the purpose of the meeting is not to problem solve; that can take place after. We also request that non-team members not be present during the meeting: The point is to ensure that team members have what they need to be effective during the day. We do, however, take action items if something needs to be escalated or followed up. I'm here to help with that process."

HOW DO WE KNOW WHEN WE'RE DONE?

The outcome of the sprint results in a work product that's customer-ready, also referred to as a *potentially shippable increment*. This is defined as having work that's been completed to the point where the features are customer-ready. The word *potential* is important here, since the end of the sprint doesn't mean that the team has completed all of its work. The point is that the team members have confidence that the hypotheses and data stories they've been working on are ready to share with their customers. For analytic teams, the potentially shippable product increment might be a data quality assessment, data profiling documentation, or analysis, for example.

The Scrum team defines "done" in advance. Having a common definition ensures that all team members and stakeholders are working with the same goal in mind. Many organizations often report that something is complete when it is really only 80 to 90 percent finished. If the meaning of "done" is clear and transparent, progress can be reported more accurately. The "definition of done" can differ for different Scrum teams and may be tied to acceptance tests, regulatory requirements, development standards, and/or stakeholder signoff. Isabel uses a consistent version of done across the analytic projects. They include their analytic quality practices as part of the criteria. They've also created a series of phase deliverables that they want to ensure are completed in every project.

SPRINT REVIEW

The sprint review provides the opportunity for the extended project team to evaluate the completed sprint output. The extended team includes the Scrum team, stakeholders, sponsors, customers, and other interested parties. Getting feedback from stakeholders is essential to ensuring the project stays on track and is viable.

Sprint review meeting preparation activities may include determining invitees, scheduling, confirming that the work is complete, and preparing a walkthrough of the work completed. The sprint review is a low-ceremony, high-value event—don't spend a lot of time preparing for it.

> "Since we do this every week," Rebecca tells the group, "we limit our sprint review to a couple of hours with only 30-60 minutes of prep. After all, you've spent all week doing the work and it's "done." We use the time to review

the data sources and to go over any analysis that might have been generated during the sprint. Most of our time is spent answering questions and making note of any changes. Sometimes the conversation around the analysis results in changes to our assumptions—we take that feedback, prioritize it, and put any new work into future sprints."

She continues. "We start the meeting by summarizing the work that was accomplished during the sprint. If there's any misalignment between the original sprint goal and the completed work, the team provides an explanation. It's not unusual in these projects to have the data take you in a new direction, but we certainly don't want to surprise any of our stakeholders. Often, it's an indicator of how we need to improve communication or understanding.

"Then the team will provide a walkthrough of its analysis—this could include reports or visualization of the information. The discussion that takes place around the analysis is the heart of the meeting—our stakeholders provide observations or commentary. It's their opportunity to ask questions and challenge us. The Scrum team benefits from a greater understanding of the work and its relevance to the business. The important rule is that sprint reviews are not used for problem solving. If we uncover a roadblock or a gap in understanding, we'll take that offline. What we really want to know at the end of our sprint is:

- Does the analysis make sense?
- Did we miss or misunderstand anything?
- Are any changes needed to the analysis?
- Should additional analysis be performed?
- Are we overanalyzing any information?

We take all of this feedback and use it as inputs into our product backlog. The review sessions also help us with backlog grooming. As we gain a better understanding through conversations with the customer, new backlog items can be created, and existing items reprioritized or removed."

SPRINT RETROSPECTIVE

The final meeting within a sprint cycle is the retrospective. The retrospective occurs after the sprint review and before the next sprint planning meeting. This meeting is attended by only the Scrum team and the product owner, and provides the group with the opportunity to evaluate the team's Scrum processes and technical practices. The outcome of the retrospective is a number of process improvement actions that will be undertaken by the team during the next sprint.

> "After the sprint review, the team decamps to the war room for our sprint retrospective. We keep the meeting to about 30 minutes. Each team member answers two questions: What went well during our sprint? What could be improved in the next sprint? I collect the feedback and we create action items that can be implemented during the next sprint. Often, these action items are included within the product backlog. Sometimes our action items are related to the team's process. Things that we can't immediately address go into an insight backlog. This is a tool the entire analytic organization uses to define and reshape our analytic practices."

After the retrospective, nothing is more critical than following through on action items. To ensure follow-up, coordinate with the product owner and make sure that the items go on the product backlog. Team members should take accountability for following through.

SUMMARY

Sprints are timeboxed, consistent-duration cycles of development work. Each sprint contains four inspect-and-adapt activities: planning, execution, review, and retrospective. Sprint planning includes setting a sprint goal and selecting high priority work aligned to that goal from the product backlog. Backlog items are decomposed into a set of development tasks. The team determines how the work will be executed. During sprint execution, the Scrum team meets each day for a daily standup meeting. The meeting is used to keep the team on track and informed of progress and barriers. At the end of the sprint, the extended project team meets for a sprint review. The review session allows stakeholders to evaluate the completed sprint output and provide feedback. After the review, the Scrum team holds a retrospective to identify areas of improvement in the team's Scrum process.

CHAPTER 8

Analytic Scrum Roles and Responsibilities

The team is the most important component of the Scrum framework, and its goal is simple: Deliver value to the customer. One of the fundamental differences in the agile development team approach is the focus on people skills over role definition. Scrum development teams self-organize around the work to be done and are cross-functional in nature. They are responsible for determining how the work is done and self-manage as the work is being performed.

As we noted earlier, the Scrum team composition is surprisingly simple, comprised of three key functions: the product owner (or sponsor), ScrumMaster, and the development team. The product owner determines what features the product will contain and the sequence for developing those features. The ScrumMaster guides the team in following Scrum processes. The development determines how features will be delivered based on the product owner's guidance. While there may be additional roles on your particular Scrum team, these are the three required roles within the Scrum framework. Figure 8.1 outlines people and process considerations for defining your new analytic Scrum team.

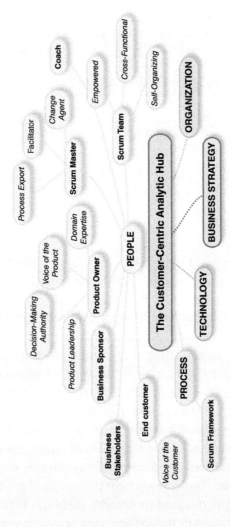

Figure 8.1 Analytic Scrum Role and Responsibility Considerations

PRODUCT OWNER DESCRIPTION

In a typical Scrum project, the product owner provides the central point of product leadership and retains single authority for determining the features and functionality that will be built within the system and the order for the development of the functionality. In this leadership role, the product owner maintains and communicates the product vision to the stakeholders and the Scrum team, and owns the ultimate success of the project deliverables. Product owners are responsible for the work effort of the team and their results. The Scrum team has an obligation to provide the product owner with all the information she needs to make good business decisions.

The product owner plays a critical role on two fronts. The product owner (1) balances the needs and priorities of the organization, customers, and end users; and (2) gives a single voice to the project, providing guidance to the development team on the functionality that needs to be delivered to satisfy stakeholder needs. The product owner drives the validation and verification process for determining that project outputs are satisfactorily delivered. In an analytic project, the product owner responsibility is primary to provide project leadership and support in the form of a more traditional project sponsor role (see Figure 8.2).

As the project sponsor, additional responsibilities include making economic decisions at different points during the development cycle. Sponsors help the team make trade-offs in scope, timelines, costs, and quality during the project as new information is gathered. An

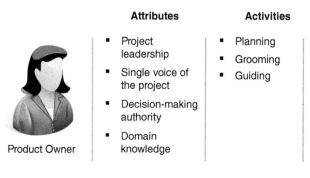

Figure 8.2 The Product Owner

example trade-off might be an opportunity to add in new data sources during the middle of the project that might dramatically increase predictability, but that result in a schedule slip. The team might even find information or insights that change the direction or viability of the project. The product owner/sponsor oversees this decision-making process.

At the end of each iteration or sprint, the product owner/sponsor also makes the determination on whether to continue funding the project. If the team is making good progress on the goal, or the continuation of development is economically viable, the next iteration will be funded. Funding for the project may be cancelled in the event that the model output meets its goals earlier than expected. An example would be a project with 10 planned iterations. After several iterations, the product owner reviews the remaining items in the product backlog and determines that the cost of development isn't worth the additional functionality. Releasing the results early may make more sense.

The product owner plays a critical role in portfolio, product, release, and sprint-planning activities. At the portfolio level, the product owner works with internal stakeholders and approval or governance committees to ensure the product is positioned within the organization's portfolio backlog. As product-planning work commences, the product owner works with stakeholders and customers to create a product vision. At the release level, the product owner works with the stakeholders and development team to prioritize what output or analysis fits within a release cycle. Finally, as part of sprint planning, the product owner assists the team in defining the sprint goal.

The product owner is responsible for overseeing the "grooming" of the product backlog, which represents features and functionality not yet developed. Grooming responsibilities include creating, refining, and prioritizing backlog items. The analytic development team performs the estimating with input or clarification from the product owner.

The product owner retains responsibility for defining product backlog item acceptance criteria. The acceptance criteria represent the conditions under which the product owner is satisfied that requirements have been met. The product owner may write the acceptance criteria, but more frequently may enlist subject matter experts or expert users to assist with the process. Acceptance criteria should be verified during sprint execution, not during the sprint review. When capabilities are tested during the development process, the product owner can help identify mistakes and/or gaps in understanding. This illustrates why product owners must have domain knowledge: They need to have a deep understanding of the business domain so that they can guide the analytic team as questions arise.

The product owner collaborates closely with the analytic development team and internal/external (i.e., customers) during the sprint. The product owner, as the voice of the customer, represents internal and external stakeholder needs and values. The product owner engages with these stakeholders to gather input and synthesize a consistent vision for the product.

Many organizations that begin to adopt Scrum often fail to encourage the right level of product owner engagement with the development team. In the traditional "waterfall" development model, customer engagement is high up front and then at the end of the project. In Scrum, product owner engagement is high, consistent, and level throughout the project. This helps mitigate the risk of creating a deliverable that doesn't meet customer needs.

For the Scrum team, this means that it will be challenging to get the product owner's dedication and time during sprint cycles. However, this participation is essential to the project—without the product owner's guidance, the Scrum team will not have a clear sense of priorities and may be working on the wrong capabilities.

Product Owner: A Day in the Life

"You want me to do what?" exclaims Sherry. "I barely have enough time to manage my organization, let alone spend all my time on this project. Can't you just email me a status report like everyone else?"

"This is a really important role for your project," says Isabel, "but we also understand that you're really busy. You can delegate someone else from your organization, but that person must have decision-making authority and a solid understanding of your business. After all, the output of this project could have a big impact on how your organization does its work today. But if you delegate, we need to ensure that you're carving out the time for that person to be an active participant on the team. Look, the product owner doesn't have to sit with the team all week—we just need his or her input during our Friday review and planning sessions. It's about a half-day commitment per week."

"That's not so bad. I have a leader on my team who really understands the work that we do. He also told me that he was really interested in this project." Sherry thinks for a minute. "But how do I ensure that I'm getting up-to-date information from your organization?"

"We have an executive steering committee that meets monthly. Since your initiative is part of our strategic projects, we review at an executive level. We also have working committee meetings each week for the broader organization. I believe your team has representation there as well. If you'd like, I can have Rebecca send you a brief status report each week after the sprint review."

"I think that will work," says Sherry. "I'll give Jim a heads up that you'll be coordinating this project with him. If we find that I need to be more involved down the road, we can work that out."

SCRUMMASTER DESCRIPTION

The ScrumMaster is a Scrum process expert, facilitator, and coach. Unlike a traditional project management role, the ScrumMaster does not define and control the team's work, but empowers the team to determine how the work is accomplished. The ScrumMaster is a servant-leader whose objective is to help the team be more effective (see Figure 8.3).

In the role as process lead, the ScrumMaster ensures that the Scrum team understands and embraces Scrum values. The Scrum-Master helps the team and the organization develop their own specific Scrum approach and facilitates the change management process in ensuring adoption of Scrum practices. The ScrumMaster helps the team continuously improve and align to its development practices.

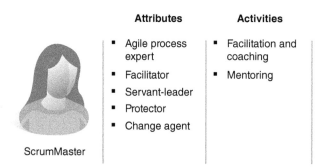

	Attributes	Activities
	■ Agile process expert	■ Facilitation and coaching
	■ Facilitator	■ Mentoring
	■ Servant-leader	
	■ Protector	
	■ Change agent	
ScrumMaster		

Figure 8.3 The ScrumMaster

As a team facilitator and coach, the ScrumMaster helps remove impediments to the team's progress and productivity, and assists in making improvement to the team's Scrum process. ScrumMasters coach both the development team and the product owner on an individual and whole-team basis. From Lyssa Adkins (2010), "Coaching helps the team's performance get better, in a series of steps coached by you and chosen by them. Mentoring transfers your agile knowledge and experience to the team as that specific knowledge becomes relevant to what's happening with them." The ScrumMaster enables the team to achieve higher levels of performance by helping team members work through any challenges that arise during the development process.

ScrumMasters protect their teams from outside interference so the team can stay focused on the task at hand. Outside interference can come from internal and external stakeholders (e.g., a vice president comes into team's space in the middle of a sprint and asks for additional features). The ScrumMaster intercepts interference and resolves issues that might interfere with the team's progress.

The ScrumMaster facilitates the removal of impediments to the team's productivity. Impediments can include problems outside of the team's control (e.g, dependencies on other projects or teams). If the team cannot remove the impediment, the ScrumMaster should take ownership of working with those other teams to remove the impediment.

ScrumMasters change minds! As with any new process, there are cultural challenges in adopting Scrum within the organization. As change agent, the ScrumMaster may be responsible for communicating and championing the value of Scrum within the organization.

ScrumMaster: A Day in the Life

"How did I get to be a ScrumMaster? Well, that's a funny story," says Rebecca. "Like a lot of people, I just fell into the role. Before I joined Isabel's team, I was working as a project manager in our IT department. We were having a lot of trouble executing on some large projects and the organization wanted to try some new approaches to see if we could improve our delivery capabilities. When the IT group was piloting Scrum, I jumped on board. We had some good successes and the rest of the organization started to notice. I was already evangelizing to some of the other teams out there—showing them how they could start to use Scrum in their business projects. Isabel saw me give a lunch-and-learn presentation to our marketing team. We met later and he wanted to know if I'd help him figure out how Scrum might apply to analytic projects. Lo-and-behold, here I am!

"My particular role is a bit of a hybrid. After being a ScrumMaster on several analytic projects, I took a broader role in managing the analytic team's portfolio. We use agile there, too. I've got two other ScrumMasters who are dedicated to the team; they also have dual roles where they help the team members with their documentation and other outputs in addition to facilitating the Scrum process on our larger projects.

"What skills do I think a ScrumMaster needs to have?" She pauses. "First, it's helpful to understand what the team does. I don't have to be an expert in analytics or any of the technologies we use, but I've got to know the basics. Second, you can't be a control freak—you have to facilitate and you have to collaborate. Remember that it's not about you; it's about the team. Third, you have to be strong enough to help protect the team from distractions. This is why we created the working committee structure for our stakeholders—all requests for the team's time are funneled through a centralized intake system. This ensures we've got the right resources working on the right projects.

Fourth, we ensure that the team follows the practices that they agreed upon. If we find that certain practices have become irrelevant, we have a mechanism for addressing that. We certainly don't want people wasting time on work that doesn't add value. And finally, you need a big dose of patience. Part of the role is helping the team members come to their own conclusions and find solutions to problems. You can't solve every problem on your own."

ANALYTIC DEVELOPMENT TEAM DESCRIPTION

Unlike other methodologies that define specific development roles, the Scrum development team incorporates a variety of roles based on the requirements of the project. Our team could include modelers, coders, architects, ETL specialists, testers, and business analysts, encompassing a diverse, cross-functional group of resources (see Figure 8.4).

Agile teams are self-organizing: This means that it's up to the team to determine how the work will be performed. Typical teams are between five and nine people, and collectively the group must have the skills needed to complete the work. Since quality is a key component of the analytic development process (and owned by the team), a Scrum team will typically not have a separate quality-testing role.

The cross-functional development team is responsible for "grooming" the backlog: The process of grooming includes creating, refining, estimating, and prioritizing product backlog items. While the product owner selects the high-priority items for the team to work on, team members are responsible for determining what can be accomplished within the sprint.

The development team participates in sprint planning prior to the execution of each sprint. Working closely with the product owner (and facilitated by the ScrumMaster), the sprint goal is established. This process includes determining which high-priority features will be selected from the product backlog and developed during the sprint. During the sprint review, the development team, product owner, ScrumMaster, stakeholders, and customers perform a review of the features completed during the sprint. The development team reviews and improves the Scrum processes during the sprint retrospective.

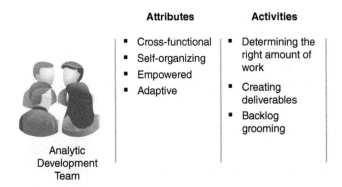

	Attributes	Activities
Analytic Development Team	■ Cross-functional ■ Self-organizing ■ Empowered ■ Adaptive	■ Determining the right amount of work ■ Creating deliverables ■ Backlog grooming

Figure 8.4 Development Team Attributes

Based on their experience through a number of large analytic projects, Isabel had a good sense of what roles were needed full-time versus part-time.

"So you're not going to know until you get through a few of these projects which roles beyond the analytic skillset are going to be important," she says. "When we started down this path, we begged, borrowed, and stole resources from other teams. As we started to identify the practices that made the projects successful, it gave us a better idea of what resources we needed full-time versus part-time, and who we needed to hire and resources we could borrow. It's not a perfect process, but we've managed to make it work."

She continued, "On many of our projects, our data scientists are the jack-of-all-trades—they're doing it all, and a lot of times, that's just fine. But just because they're doing it all, it doesn't mean that they do it all well. For our larger, more strategic projects, we get more granular in the roles and bring in more specialists. For our customer retention project, we're going to bring in one of our ETL developers. Our ETL developer is an expert in optimizing the code that extracts, transforms, and loads data from source systems into our analytic environment, and can also productionalize that code so that we can meet the IT standards and service-level agreements required for operational model deployment. Sometimes we also need a database administrator, but not full-time. Our ETL developers have good relationships with that team—they know when to bring them in.

"We also recognized that our data scientists were annoyed and distracted by some of the extra practices we agreed on as a team. Most of this work is around the necessary documentation of our insight—we think it's critical to create a knowledge repository of our work and insights, but a lot of people aren't good at that kind of work. So we have some strong business analysts who support that process. It allows the data scientists to focus on the work that engages them, but allows us to institutionalize the knowledge and learnings coming out of these projects."

ADDITIONAL ROLES

While Scrum only specifies three dedicated roles (product owner, ScrumMaster, and development team), you may find several other roles that are associated with the team. Here are some additional roles you might find on an agile analytic project:

Business Sponsor While the product owner serves as the liaison between stakeholders and developers, funding comes from an executive business sponsor within the organization. This is the person or entity that provides funding for the project. The product owner is charged with execution. In our agile analytic project, we recognize that we may not have the luxury of a full-time product owner (and honestly, we might not need someone in that role full-time!), so sometimes you will have a sponsor who takes on product owner responsibilities part-time. The key to making this successful is setting expectations upfront on what the role and expectations are.

Agile Coach In Scrum, the ScrumMaster can serve as the coach. But for organizations that are just starting down the path to agile delivery or have multiple Scrum teams across multiple projects, the coach role may be separate. The coach is a process and enablement expert, providing advice and best practices to the ScrumMaster and helping teams become "unstuck" for particularly tough problems. Coaching isn't just for project administration: This person may have a technical lead role on the project, providing expertise to more junior resources on the project.

Domain Specialists Domain specialists, or SMEs, provide the deep business, functional, or system/data expertise that a development team needs to understand a domain. For example, in our retention analytic project, the team will need SMEs that are experienced in how the business deals with customers. From a systems and data perspective, our team might need SMEs on customer administration or other operational systems. SMEs are instrumental in guiding the team toward interpreting the data correctly. In your analytic project, your data SMEs will play a critical role and are fully engaged throughout the project. In addition to their expertise on the data, they will be able to guide the team around the feasibility of possible solutions.

Business Analysts The business analyst role augments the development effort by bridging the communication and requirements gap often experienced between business stakeholders and the development team. While the analyst doesn't replace the customer role on the project, the analyst can assist in translating customer needs into development tasks. In Isabel's organization, the ScrumMasters have dual business analyst skills. In addition to supporting the team through the Scrum process, they may assist in capturing and disseminating project information.

Testers In Scrum, the testing role is embedded within the development team as part of the team's quality practices. For larger projects where analytics might be embedded into an operational system, testing functions may be separate. This doesn't relieve the data scientists from delivering error-free code, but provides a separate line of defense for ensuring high-quality, bug-free deliverables.

SUMMARY

Remember that the most important part of the Scrum process is the team, and its purpose is to deliver value to the customer. Scrum teams have three primary roles: the product owner, the Scrum team, and the ScrumMaster. Product owners provide product leadership and are accountable to the business and end-customers of the product. The Scrum team executes on the product vision in short iterative cycles. Scrum teams are self-organizing and cross-functional. The ScrumMaster is the Scrum process authority, and ensure that the team is adhering to Scrum processes. The ScrumMaster also protects the team from outside interruptions, so the team can focus on high-quality deliverables. In addition to the three key roles, a number of other roles may exist internally and externally to the team, depending on the agile methodology used or other organizational requirements.

CHAPTER **9**

Gathering Analytic User Stories

s you now know, agile analytics projects don't attempt to predict or plan every possible requirement in advance, but they do have a structure that keeps the team's eye on the goal. Team members make decisions with the information they have at the time and then reviews and revalidates that information (and takes in new information!) throughout the project. When using an agile framework, the team doesn't invest a lot of time or effort in gathering all of the details up front. In an agile analytic project, that's not possible most of the time anyway—the insights you find along the way help define the next steps (see Figure 9.1).

OVERVIEW

If we were going to use a waterfall project management methodology, we'd gather requirements in a series of lengthy requirements sessions at the start of our project, take a lot of notes, and write up a bunch of requirement documents that no one would ever look at. What's worse is that those documents would likely become irrelevant

Figure 9.1 Analytic User Story Considerations

very quickly: Throughout the project duration, business needs almost always change or need refinement. Change in a waterfall project is generally discouraged; after all, if someone changes his or her mind after the team has completed a lot of work, that can result in rework. In this case, change would be managed through a complex change management process that has the impact of discouraging change (possibly because the process itself is too complex, restrictive, or punitive). The unfortunate result is that at the end of the project, the insights that are delivered might not be relevant or appropriate for the desired business outcome. Since we did all of our planning work upfront, the lack of frequent customer feedback loops pulled the project off track.

Many analytic teams don't engage enough with their stakeholders and may not even be capturing formal requirements at all. In any project management discipline, waterfall or agile, understanding and documenting your customers' needs and ensuring they're part of the project team is critical.

Defining requirements requires equal participation from people who can see the project from both the technology and business perspective. When participation is unbalanced, business functionality is often defined with little thought to technology practicality, or the modelers may define a solution that is technically or analytically perfect, but may not meet business needs (or doesn't make sense!). If you continuously engage with your stakeholders through the analytic process, you're more likely to have a better, more business-viable outcome.

USER STORIES

In an agile project, requirements are captured in the form of "user stories." A user story represents some functionality that will be valuable to an end user. User stories are composed of three elements (Cohn, 2004), as highlighted in Figure 9.2:

- A written description of the story used for planning and a reminder (the "card")
- Conversations about the story that serve to provide story details (the "conversation")
- Acceptance tests that document details that are used to determine story completeness (the "confirmation")

In the agile world, user stories are documented on hand-written note cards (or in your agile project management tool) and made visible to the entire project team (see Figure 9.3). The purpose of using a notecard is to keep the story contained and to serve as a representation, not documentation, of a customer requirement. A user story is not a contractual obligation. The conversation helps ensure that the requirements are properly discussed and communicated; it also provides fast feedback, facilitating a shared understanding of the business requirement.

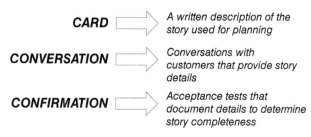

CARD ⇨ *A written description of the story used for planning*

CONVERSATION ⇨ *Conversations with customers that provide story details*

CONFIRMATION ⇨ *Acceptance tests that document details to determine story completeness*

A user story represents functionality that will be valuable to the end user

Figure 9.2 The Card, the Conversation, and the Confirmation
Source: Cohn (2004)

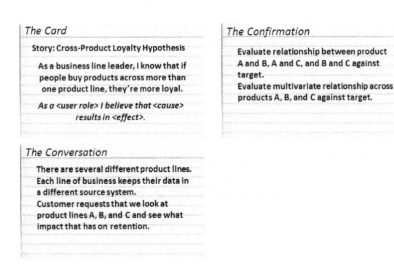

Figure 9.3 Analytic User Story in Action

You might ask yourself: *How do I write a user story for an analytic project? After all, I'm not developing software.* Just think of user stories as a great way to collect and express customer needs and desires simply. Frame analytic user stories around questions that stakeholders would like analyzed or hypotheses that need to be tested. In fact, a great approach is to capture all of the things that your business community thinks they know about the problem that you're trying to solve. This will help you define which data sources to evaluate and how to structure the data for the analysis.

The Card

For most co-located teams, index cards or sticky notes are still a common way to capture user stories (for team members on distributed agile teams, agile project management tools are nice for keeping things organized). The small format of the card keeps the team from eliciting too much detail. The standard user story template includes a user role, an outline of what that the user wants to achieve, and why that capability is important to the user: "As a <user role> I want to <goal> so that <benefit>." The purpose of using a small notecard is to keep requirements and assumptions from becoming too detailed. The card should simply capture the essence or intent of the requirement.

As an example, in our retention project, we'll start capturing all of the hypotheses around what makes people leave. For analytic projects, we'll change the format of the user story to: "As a <user role> I believe that <cause> results in <effect>."

Analytic User Story Examples

For your analytic project, spend time with your business partners to perform a little root cause analysis. By validating or negating their assumptions throughout the project, you'll ensure greater buy-in with the results. You'll also have a great starting point for identifying the data sources that will be important inputs into the project. Stories aren't just for business stakeholders to define: The modelers will create and test a number of their own assumptions as well.

> As a marketer, I believe that our lack of product innovation causes customers to look elsewhere.
>
> As a call center rep, customers are telling me that they're leaving because they don't use our product anymore.
>
> As a product developer, I've seen new competitors offer alternative products that are appealing to customers.
>
> As a call center rep, when customers go to renew our service, they are sometimes surprised by the bill and they don't renew.
>
> As a marketer, I think that we send out too many messages to our customers; they're tired of hearing from us and they're not listening to our messages.
>
> As a business line leader, I know that if people buy products across more than one product line, they're more loyal.
>
> As an eCommerce lead, I believe that people who use our website are more loyal than those who buy our products in a store.

Technical User Stories

If you've done any reading on user stories, the prevailing mindset is that all user stories should reflect value to an end customer. Purists argue that technical user stories don't add business value. However, user stories have heavy dependencies on technical architecture and infrastructure. Your product owner/sponsor needs to understand the impact and trade-offs between the analysis that the team is going to perform and the infrastructure necessary to support it (either short- or long-term).

That said, be judicious about the inclusion of technical user stories, and try and frame them in a way that the business will understand the value and need to prioritize them. This can include the purchase of new hardware, software or databases, upgrades to existing environments, and additional information security provisions. You will, however, want to recognize any technical implications that may delay work throughout the project.

One way to get around having too many technical stories in your backlog is to take care of them before you even start your project. Ensure that as many of the components that you need to perform your work are set up in advance. However, as you progress through the project, you might find you need a new piece of software or need some training on a new technique. These are elements that can be captured as stories and prioritized on an ongoing basis.

Example technical user stories might be:

- As an analyst, I need Hadoop infrastructure to store and access web data so that the information can be analyzed.
- As an analyst, I need training on Pig and Hive programming languages so that I can work with data in Hadoop.
- As an analyst, we need access to a sandbox environment to work with the data so that our work will not impact other users.
- As the IT department, we need to upgrade the DBMS to the latest version so that we can receive vendor support.

Again, do the best you can to frame these stories in a way that is valuable to the end customer. For these types of stories, follow the user, goal, and benefit structure of a standard user story.

The Conversation

Story details are elicited through additional conversations and dialogues between the analytic team and stakeholders. These conversations take place through the life of the user story, from the initial capture, refinement, estimation, planning, and review processes. The conversations lead to additional notes for your story that add context, including available data sources, business rules, and organizational constraints.

Following our ABP example, as the analysts have a conversation with the eCommerce team, they learn more about the web data sources. It turns out that they can only track customer online when they sign in and authenticate; so while they can track purchases, they can't identify other online customer activity. In a subsequent conversation with the retail team, they discover that they don't have any way to track customers who made cash purchases. The analytic team documents the data sources that can be evaluated to look at some cross-channel purchases, but also notes the limitation of the data.

Think of your limitations as future opportunities. Create an idea backlog to capture limitations in the data or business processes as possible future projects for the organization.

The Confirmation

The user story also contains confirmation in the form of acceptance tests that clarify the behavior of the requirement. This helps the development team understand the criteria on which to build the analysis. This information is captured on the back of the card. A confirmation could be something as simple as evaluating or profiling a data set associated with that story, or a more robust statistical assumption.

The tests on the back of the story card are geared toward customer acceptance. Think of it as, "Yes, I proved the relationship; or no, I didn't." The team may have many more technical tests associated with the story that are transparent to the customer.

Possible tests for our eCommerce user story might include:

- Evaluate web transaction logs.
- Evaluate retail data sources.

- Evaluate relationship between cross-channel purchases and retention.

Acceptance tests allow the team to verify that the story has been completed. The customers define the test in the form of their hypothesis. As you bring the customer results, you may form additional hypotheses that can be captured as additional user stories. The process of developing acceptance tests is iterative; additional tests may be added to the story prior to development. As new details are identified, tests may be added.

In our retention, our user story may have the following acceptance tests that help us add detail and context. Note that the acceptance tests might be categorized as statistical tests:

- Test customers with eCommerce transactions with all retail transactions.
- Test customers with eCommerce transactions against retail Product A.
- Test customers with eCommerce transactions against retail Product B.
- Test customers with eCommerce customers against non-eCommerce customers.
- Run multivariate analysis on all product combinations for each customer and see what shakes out.

As always, use your best judgment to define the level of detail that you want to capture. You don't want to spend more time writing notes on cards than you are performing analysis.

TOOLS AND TECHNIQUES

Agile teams require the continuous participation and interaction of both the customers and the developers throughout the life of the project. While the process of capturing user stories is a group activity requiring the participation of customers and the development team, the customer is responsible for writing the stories. This is designed to keep the story focused in the language of the business. It also allows the customer to take ownership of the product and assists the customer team in prioritizing stories for iterations and releases.

Stories can be written at any time during the project, but an initial set of stories may be captured in a story-writing workshop at the start of the project. Additional techniques for capturing user stories include conducting interviews with end users, questionnaires or surveys, and monitoring/observation. As you're gathering your stories, use a variety of techniques.

The team may group stories into a product roadmap and perform some initial prioritization. The analytic team will take the first set of high-priority stories and begin to estimate the work effort.

INVEST IN GOOD STORIES

Characteristics of a good user story can be defined by the INVEST acronym (Wake, 2003). Since the INVEST method is widely used as a guideline for user story development, standard descriptions are shown. However, it's necessary to tweak them a little so that they are relevant to analytic user stories, as shown in Table 9.1.

Getting the hang of writing good user stories is an art, and it will likely take your team a few iterations to capture the information needed to begin development work. Cohn (2004) points out some story "smells" (as in, if something stinks, it probably needs to be fixed):

Watch out for stories that are too small. They might cause problems with scheduling and estimation. Look for opportunities to combine stories where you can identify interdependencies.

Interdependencies will also cause problems with iteration planning. If the stories are small, combine them; if they are large or right-sized, try and split into layers of functionality.

Don't "gold-plate" your analysis. In our analytic projects, overanalysis can cause troubles. Only do what is required to complete the story. If your customers ask you for additional analysis later (or if you find something that's really interesting!), you can capture that as an additional story for the product backlog.

Avoid too many upfront details. This can be challenging for teams that are just switching over to agile methodologies from waterfall. The purpose of using a notecard to capture a story is to keep the amount of detail to a minimum. Remember—it's a reminder to have a conversation, not create documentation.

Table 9.1 INVEST Attributes for Analytics

Attribute	Description	Implications for Analytics
I = INDEPENDENT	Stories should not overlap in concept so that they can be scheduled or implemented in any order.	In analytic projects, overlapping stories are fine since the data sources you're using to answer different questions will be the same. We recommend instead categorizing your stories by the data sources that you'll be analyzing.
N = NEGOTIABLE	Details are created by both the customer and developer during the development period. A user story will capture the spirit of the feature, not the details. As the team begins work, additional information or clarification will be added, but it is not necessary for prioritization.	Capture what you need to know and validate (or not) any assumptions, but don't exhaustively try and capture the story. Let the data do the talking.
V = VALUABLE	The story must be valuable to the customer. Developer concerns must be framed so that customers or end-users can understand the value. Avoid stories that are only valuable to developers.	Frame your user stories around hypotheses. Avoid user stories that focus on statistical, technical, or architectural details.
E = ESTIMABLE	The story needs to be the right size for a high-level estimation, which will assist the customer in prioritizing where the story will fit in during an implementation.	One of the challenges faced by analytic teams is the unknown aspects of many data sources that will be used in the project. This makes estimation a challenge. But if the team can group analytic projects by data source dependency, then once the data is available, the work becomes estimable. This will be covered in more detail in our chapter on Estimation.

Table 9.1 (continued)

Attribute	Description	Implications for Analytics
S = SMALL	A story will generally encompass no more than a few weeks (or days) of work effort. Smaller stories tend to be more estimable.	As the team works through its estimation process, bigger-than-a-breadbox user stories will pop out (imagine a story for our retention project that says, "The our website has a huge impact on retention"). If this is an important discovery area for the project, the team will work to break that story—called an epic—into more manageable analyses.
T = TESTABLE	The test is critical in ensuring that the feature/functionality delivers as expected. Stories without tests may be often poorly defined or understood by customers.	Analytics are a little different in that hypothesis tests are important in validating business assumptions. On the other hand, you don't want to lose site of interesting insights that people didn't anticipate—these should be exploited.

EPICS

When a story gets too big, it becomes an epic. In our retention project, one of the stakeholders says: "Hey, I know if customers use our website they're less likely to churn." Think about all of the things customers can do on the web—they can look for information, browse products, buy products, check their account, and more. There are many details that need to be addressed, and they can be broken down into smaller stories, such as:

- Customers who register on our website are more likely to remain customers.
- Customers who buy products on the website are more likely to remain customers.
- Customers who browse frequently on the website are more likely to remain customers.

The point is not to plan for every single detail or contingency, but provide the right level of detail for planning. In fact, epics don't need to be broken down until the team is ready for the story in an iteration planning cycle. Keep in mind that the user story serves as a "conversation" point between the end users and the developers, and the conversation is had when the details become important. Too much detail written into the story may imply that no further discussion is needed, when in fact the opposite may be true. An epic provides a good overview of what the project is about, but it's too big to work on. The next size stories might be classified as features, but are still too big to be completed within an iteration. When the stories get to the level where the team can estimate the work effort in days, then they're at the right size to begin working on. The final breakdown of the story is the task, which can be estimated in hours and completed by one or two people. Most likely, your analytic stories are fine without significant task detail unless there's a dependency on another team or resource to complete some of the work.

SUMMARY

Functionality for your analytic project can be described in the form of a user story: a written description of the requirement from an end user perspective. Analytic stories capture questions and hypotheses the business has around the analytic objective. Story workshops provide a good starting point for capturing a set of initial questions, but remember that additional stories can be added and prioritized at any point in the project.

User stories reflect functionality valued by end users. Include technical stories, but frame them in a way that the business understands the value and importance of the story. Analytic stories should reflect characteristics outlined by the INVEST attributes, but adapt them for your particular project. Stories that represent too much functionality are known as epics. Epics can be decomposed into smaller stories as the team begins a planning cycle. Finally, acceptance tests round out the story and provide the team with details that confirm story completeness.

CHAPTER 10

Facilitating Your Story Workshop

If you've got a brand new analytic project you're working on that's new for the business, identifying stakeholders across the organization helps the team get their bearings on which resources will be critical to the project. Understanding the stakeholders' impression of the project and their level of influence helps you get in front of people who may negatively impact the project (or positively help it!). Once you've identified the resources that can provide valuable input, prepare for your story workshop (see Figure 10.1). Use brainstorming techniques to run your meeting, capture and organize their ideas, and always follow up with your participants.

STAKEHOLDER ANALYSIS

Analytic projects, especially the ones that will likely have a large business impact, have business stakeholders. It's critical to identify the right people upfront and engage them through the project. These are the people who are closest to the business—their experience and intuition provide important inputs to overall context of the project. Their guidance on what's appropriate in a business context is also crucial: They can give analysts a much-needed reality check for the business validity of the

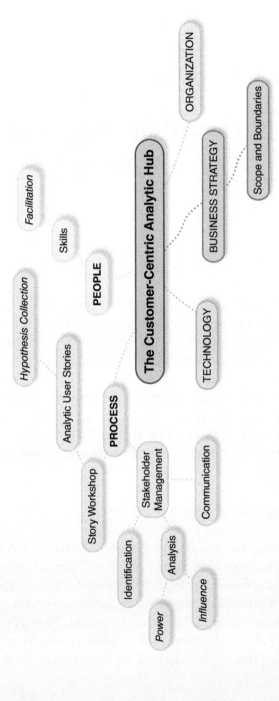

Figure 10.1 Story Workshop Considerations

statistical output. Another reason for engaging with them throughout the process is that these are the teams that will be acting on the output of your model. If they don't understand how the analysts came to their conclusions or think that the team missed information that should have been analyzed, the rollout of your results will be in jeopardy.

The first question you might ask is: *How do I know who should be a stakeholder?* Stakeholders are anyone with an interest in the outcome of your project. Stakeholders can be internal or external. They exist at multiple levels of the organization, and they have different levels of authority and influence.

> Rebecca begins planning a user story workshop so that the analytic group can start identifying all of the business needs and assumptions that are inputs to the analysis. Before she creates the agenda and schedules the workshop, she does some stakeholder analysis.
>
> "I'm trying to identify all of the groups that should be involved in this project," Rebecca says to Isabel. "I met with Sherry and she gave me a list of stakeholders. But this project is pretty big—I want to make sure we include all of the right people so that if we have some great results, our rollout will go more smoothly. I also don't want to include too many people. What do you think?"
>
> "Let's take a look at your stakeholder matrix." She hands her a piece of paper with the names of the stakeholders, their roles in the organization, and their influence on the project. "We should bring this to the steering committee," she said. "I think that some of these folks need to be highly involved, but others just informed. Why don't you create a communication plan and outline some strategies for getting these other less critical stakeholder groups up to speed? In the meantime, for our story workshop we should focus on the group that Sherry has provided."

Stakeholders need to be actively managed throughout the project. However, all stakeholders are not created equal. Stakeholder analysis is an important analytic project activity that helps the team identify the right participants to actively engage with, but also acknowledges secondary stakeholders who might need information about the project.

Depending on the importance of your project within the organization, you can spend a lot of time on this activity or a little time. If your project is going to change how the business runs and people perform their jobs, then you'll want to dedicate time to this activity. As an example, as an output of Isabel's customer retention project, we may develop a model that has retention propensity scores indicating if a customer is at high risk of defecting. That score might be included in a customer profile that a retail sales clerk or the call service representative (CSR) might see in the CRM application. If a score is at a certain threshold, the CSR or clerk might interact with the customer differently. So the CSR and clerk become important stakeholders in our project from an implementation change management perspective. If they don't believe that the score in the CRM application is valid, they may override it, making it difficult to gauge the efficacy of the model down the road.

Stakeholder analysis provides an important input in ongoing communication strategies and training and rollout plans. Once you've identified your stakeholders, define strategies for engaging with them.

MANAGING STAKEHOLDER INFLUENCE

Another important aspect of stakeholder analysis and management is understanding the influence that stakeholders may have over a project. Analytic projects in particular may not be well received by senior stakeholders who don't understand the benefits. There are still a lot of people out there that think it's all a bunch of "hocus pocus" or have been burned in the past by poorly executed and communicated projects. The challenge for the analytic team is to identify those people and understand their levels of influence and the need for their support.

Take the time in your stakeholder analysis to identify these people along with an assessment of their power/influence over the project, as well as an indicator of how the project will impact them. In our example in Figure 10.2, Sherry, our sponsor, is high power/influence and will be highly impacted by the project, but she is also very supportive. One of her supervisors, James Madison, doesn't have a lot of power but has some influence (he definitely has Sherry's ear!), and there will be some impact to his team. He believes that everything is just fine

Stakeholder Analysis

Key Stakeholder	Role in Organization	Power / Influence Category	Impact of Project on Stakeholder (H.M.L)	Current / Desired Support			Reasons for Resistance or Support
				Opposed	Neutral	Supportive	
Sherry Smith	VP Operations	A	H			O	Project sponsor; believes that analytics will help with customer retention
James Madison	Supervisor	B	M	O ⟶			Doesn't believe that project will positively impact his team

- Will the outcome reflect the concerns of our customers and it what the customer really wants?
- If we asked each team member what the project is for, would they provide the same ansser?
  - How importanta is the project to key stakeholders?

Figure 10.2 Stakeholder Analysis Considerations

the way it is and that this project is a waste of time. You will want to spend more time with him to understand his concerns and determine how to keep him positively engaged. Your engagement strategy for your stakeholder groups will differ based on your analysis.

AGILE VERSUS TRADITIONAL STAKEHOLDER MANAGEMENT

In agile, a select group of stakeholders (business customers) will be active participants on the project team. They will provide input into the different types of analysis they'd like done and will participate in project review sessions by providing feedback. In an agile project, there's a role dedicated to product ownership: The idea is that there is one senior person who interfaces with the external business community and gathers and prioritizes ideas as they come in. This insulates the project team from being hit with informal requests coming in from all over the place. The reality is that this model may not work on your analytic project, since you may not have a dedicated product owner. In our retention project, Sherry is our project sponsor and the de facto product owner, but that doesn't mean she has the time to go out and socialize the results and get feedback from the broader organization.

In that event, active stakeholder engagement becomes the responsibility of the project manager or ScrumMaster, a role we'll discuss in the next chapter. Don't leave out or neglect this important activity—the success of your project can depend on it.

THE STORY WORKSHOP

Once you know who the key stakeholders are, set up a story workshop to capture the initial set of requirements. The story workshop is simply a brainstorming activity used for idea generation. Your goal should be to capture as many stories as possible. You may get some crazy ideas or assumptions. That's okay. Just write them all down. Some stories might be small and simple, and others more "pie in the sky." Don't prioritize anything at this point, and don't worry if you don't capture everything. Remember, the point about agility is that the requirements can evolve over time—stakeholders may have new ideas that come to mind, or the analytic team may generate insight during their data analysis that makes people ask new questions.

Workshop Preparation

As a rule of thumb, try not to have more than 10 or so people at your first workshop. In fact, if you can limit the group to no more than five subject matter experts (SMEs), you'll have a better session. This can be a challenge to coordinate, since you might have a lot of enthusiastic stakeholders who want to add their two cents. But keep your first meeting small, and then validate the stories that you've captured with additional stakeholders as appropriate. Smaller groups are also easier to facilitate, and you'll get better input from your SMEs. If needed, you can hold another story workshop with a different group.

Key analytic team members and IT should participate as well. The analytic team can guide the SMEs in the type of data that would typically need to solve a particular type of analysis based on their experience. IT resources might be helpful in answering questions that arise about different data sources. Remember that the focus of this meeting is on gathering hypotheses, and not on solving for those hypotheses.

Meeting facilitation skills are important in holding an effective brainstorming session. This helps ensure that your group doesn't go off on tangents or problem solving. Use a "no constraint" approach—that is, think of the hypotheses that you want to ask, but don't focus on whether you have the information to answer that question today. As you get deeper into the project, you may find creative solutions to those challenges, and at a minimum, you'll be able to start creating an idea backlog for things that the organization could do in the future (get new data sources, clean up existing data sources, change business processes to enable the collection of better data, etc.).

Be sensitive to the different levels of people in the room. We've been in a lot of analytic facilitation sessions where senior leaders changed the whole atmosphere of the room and inadvertently limited discussion (or it became their discussion). People may not feel comfortable speaking up in those situations. If at all possible, try to get a read on the culture of a particular group before you set up your session—this is where your stakeholder analysis can be very helpful. If the senior leaders express an interest in attending, but you know that their presence will be disruptive, offer to meet with them after the session to walk through the stories generated by the team.

> Rebecca circles back with Isabel. "I did some recon with some of the stakeholders. Sherry has expressed an interest in attending our story workshop, but I've heard that she can be pretty dominating in meetings. For our team to get what we need to get started, we need to ensure that we've got an open flow of discussion and that we can capture a lot of different perspectives. I think it would be better if she didn't attend this session, but I could meet with her separately to review our ideas and get her input on how to prioritize. What do you think?"
>
> "I think that's a great idea," says Isabel. "Do you feel comfortable asking her that?"
>
> "Absolutely," Rebecca nods, "but I will definitely need your support."

Story workshops should also be timeboxed events. In this case, two hours will be enough to capture the initial requirements. Remember that in agile, you'll be working with your stakeholders throughout the project, not just in the beginning. Look at your first story workshop as just an initial step in shaping the direction of your analytic project. If you're facilitating the story workshop as a brainstorming session, keep it as a low-ceremony event. You want it to be constructive, but not overstructured. Try and include people who have a diverse set of experiences, skills, and thinking styles.

> Rebecca identifies the five SMEs she needs for the story workshop. Prior to setting up the meeting, she meets with each SME and provides each with an overview of the project and input that she needs from that SME. When she's ready to schedule the meeting, the SMEs are already aware of what the expectations and objectives are. She writes in the meeting invitation, "Today we're going to explore all the areas that we believe impact customer retention. Just bring your business knowledge, no preparation needed."

You might want to evaluating reports and existing analysis around your business problem, if they exist. Most organizations have exhaustively analyzed historical information that can help provide context. At a minimum, it can help guide the discussion around how your stakeholders see the problem today and available data sources to support the analysis. Reports can be good conversation starters.

Educate your attendees on what you intend to do with the information gathered and ideas generated after the meeting (or if you have any follow-ups for them). It's important that people know that the time they're investing with you will be valuable. Most people allocated to a project are doing double-duty—they've got their day-to-day jobs to worry about—so take the time to thank the attendees for their participation, and continue to highlight the organizational importance of the work that you're all doing.

Facilitating Your Workshop

If you're lucky, your participants will have tons to say around the question that you're asking them, and as a facilitator your main job will be channeling the ideas and keeping the group on track. For some facilitation sessions, you may need to use some brainstorming techniques to spur ideas and discussion.

Brainstorming can also help a group overcome *groupthink*—where everyone gravitates toward the same idea, or in situations where you have people that are either dominating the conversation or aren't speaking up. The fun part about brainstorming is that all ideas are welcome and developed upon by the team.

An effective meeting format for your brainstorming session includes:

Preparation Make sure you have a comfortable and neutral meeting room. You'll want to make sure that all of the tools you need are in the room before you start (whiteboards, markers, sticky notes, etc.). It's often difficult to facilitate and scribe at the same time, so appoint someone from the group (or bring another resource) to help capture ideas. If the group doesn't know each other well, you could introduce a warm-up exercise like an icebreaker.

Icebreaker An icebreaker is a short meeting exercise that helps the team get to know each other better. For all of the eye rolling you often get when you introduce a technique like this, I've always found it to be really effective in helping people feel more comfortable around each other, especially if this is a completely new group. Here are some short, fun activities:

Three Truths and a Lie Have each participant tell three truths and one lie about themselves. The team tries to guess which one is a lie.

Interviewing Pair up your group and have each person interview the other for five minutes. Each person will share the other person's story.

Four Quadrants Hand each person a piece of paper and divide it into four quadrants. Have participants respond to four questions by drawing a picture to represent each question. Example questions could include:

- What is your favorite car?
- Where would you like to go on vacation?
- Draw four things that do NOT describe you.
- Which famous person would you like to have dinner with?

Icebreakers are also appropriate for introducing your topic. One widely used technique is to capture "burning questions" at the start of the meeting. Capture questions your participants have about the business problem and write them on the whiteboard. Refer back to them throughout the meeting. This technique can help clarify terminology and set boundaries for the discussion. Word association icebreakers can also be used to capture an initial set of thoughts or ideas on your topic. In our retention meeting, we could ask, "What are your perceptions on retaining customers?" People could respond with answers like "happy customers," "people who like our products more," and "value for money." This is a good technique to get people going on your topic and to define the scope of the problem as appropriate.

Topic Presentation: You can use the topic icebreaker to lead into the more structured presentation of the topic, or you can jump right in. As you kick off the discussion, present the topic area to the team and the objectives of the meeting. If you're looking to generate some starting ideas, hand out pieces of paper and give people 10 to 15 minutes to write down as many ideas as they can (one idea per piece of paper). This is a good technique to get full participation from the group. Gather up the individual ideas and then walk through each one with the team. Make sure your scribe is capturing the discussion points.

As you facilitate your analytic topics, poke at people's assumptions. Someone might say: "People leave because our prices are too high." Encourage further discussion by drilling into that statement: Why are our prices too high? Is it certain products? What types of customers are saying this? Are people telling us this, or are we guessing? Again, we're looking to tease out assumptions—while your participants may have some reports to back up those assumptions, we want to gather anecdotal commentary as well. As you go through each idea, also elicit possible data sources that could be used to validate the assumption.

Try not to spend too much time on any one idea and remember to help the team stay focused. By the end of the meeting, you should have a long list of exploration areas and hypotheses for your analytic topic.

MUST-ANSWER QUESTIONS

In an analytic project, it is essential that you confirm the level of analysis that you'll be working with. In some organizations, your data may exist at the account or product level, and you need to aggregate that data to get the full picture of the customer. In other instances, you might have a primary and a secondary customer. You may also be working with households, or grouping of customers within a defined geographic space or entity. It's not unusual to find that your organization doesn't have a clear definition on what a "customer" is (or has multiple definitions), and as a result, doesn't have operational data structured appropriately to answer customer-centric questions. For example, in the insurance industry, most operational systems store information at the policy level. Is a policy a customer? What if a customer has more than one insurance policy? What if the customer is a business? These are all questions that the team should address in their story workshop.

Your goal is to create a shared understanding of the problem that you're trying to solve. Sometimes you find that that might take a little more time than you expect. Unfortunately, you might also find that the way you originally intended to do your analysis isn't feasible. In our policy example, perhaps there's no way to group records by customer with your current in-house capabilities. In that case, if it's important enough to the organization, you might stop the project and address the issue. Or if you can't overcome that constraint short-term, you might revisit the problem you're trying to solve and structure it a little differently.

In one organization, they discovered that they couldn't aggregate customer records across product lines. What they ended up doing was creating predictive models at the product level. This is actually a good iterative approach since the organization can begin to take advantage of in-product predictions, while working toward merging the product lines together. Make these decisions based on what your organizational objectives and constraints are (maybe it's okay to not have a cross-organizational customer view) and adjust your strategy as appropriate. The point is not to use barriers as an excuse: You are agile, after all.

POST-WORKSHOP

As a follow-up step, group your stories by themes, as shown in Table 10.1. You may have a series of hypotheses around the relationship between customer retention and products. The information needed to support this analysis might be stored across multiple databases or source systems. As you gather different groups of hypotheses, you can identify high-impact data sources that should be analyzed first. This helps guide the creation and prioritization of the stories.

As you gather your story themes, look for common data sources. Often, you can use the availability of data to help in the prioritization. That is, start with more easily accessible sources and then layer in addition sources over time. In our retention project, everything centers on

Table 10.1 Capturing Initial Hypotheses

Customer-Product Hypotheses
Customers who purchase products more frequently stay longer.
Customers who buy products across product categories stay longer.
Customers who buy products across channels stay longer.

Data Subject Areas	Subject Matter Experts
Customer, product, retail transactions, web transactions, channel preferences, third-party customer attributes and demographics, call center data	Jason Chu, call center Meredith Singer, eCommerce BethAnn Lewis, Retail Jeffrey Jones, Product Line 1 Michael Smith, Product Line 2 Sally McKenzie, IT Operations

the customer, so all of the customer-related tables will be the team's starting point.

After the initial hypotheses have been gathered, Rebecca prepares a summary of the hypotheses collected in the meeting grouped by data theme and aligns them by data subject area, as shown in Table 10.2.

Table 10.2 Hypothesis-Data Matrix

	Customer Data	Web Data	Product Line 1	Product Line 2	Call Center	Customer Survey	Retail Transaction
Hypothesis 1	X			X	X		X
Hypothesis 2	X	X					
Hypothesis 3	X			X	X		
Hypothesis 4	X	X	X	X	X		
Hypothesis 5	X				X	X	X
Hypothesis 6	X						X
Hypothesis 7	X	X			X	X	
Hypothesis 8	X	X	X	X			X
Hypothesis 9	X	X					X
Hypothesis 10	X		X		X		X
Hypothesis 11	X						X
TOTAL	11	5	3	4	6	2	7

This list provides a starting point for Sherry to prioritize the ideas, and for identifying high-priority data areas to analyze.

Keep in mind that at this point, we're not identifying any specific data sources or tables. We're also not looking at the feasibility of gathering the data. We're just identifying what subject areas are most useful to start analyzing first.

SUMMARY

Before you start capturing your analytic user stories, identify the stakeholders for your project. In addition to providing experience and context to the business problem that you're solving for, they play an important role in the rollout and adoption of your solutions. Stakeholder analysis helps to classify which individuals are supportive (or not) of your project. Developing strategies for communicating and managing these stakeholders based on their support is a critical analytic project activity. When you are ready to facilitate your first story workshop, use your stakeholder analysis to find the right attendees. Prepare for your meeting by selecting some brainstorming tools to help the team generate ideas. Ideas can be grouped by data themes and used to help prioritize your hypotheses by relevant data areas.

CHAPTER 11

Collecting
Knowledge
Through Spikes

Quite often, a team might be faced with a new architecture, design, or technology that it must assess or explore before team members can begin to work on their project. Within agile, this exploratory activity is called a *spike,* although terms such as prototype, proof-of-concept, and experiment are also appropriate. The spike is a small, timeboxed experiment that helps the team better understand what they're working with. In analytic projects, data spikes are useful in providing a high-level assessment of what information is available and the quality of it. As you start your data spike, engage with your business and IT partners early. In Figure 11.1 we can see that data knowledge gathering considerations are complex: In addition to identifying what data sources exist, we need to find the people that understand the quality of the data, and can identify ways to extract it.

WITH DATA, WELL BEGUN IS HALF DONE

One of the biggest barriers in analytics—regardless of the analytic maturity in your organization—is the time needed to collect, access,

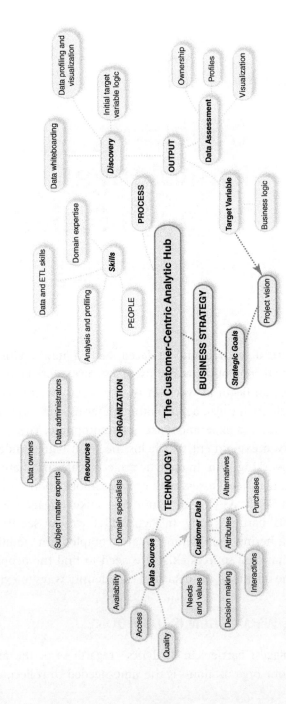

Figure 11.1 Data Knowledge Gathering Considerations

and assess the data. As an example, one analytics group assigned six people to a project to collect and assess the data: It took them six months to conclude that they were missing critical data, which resulted in the team abandoning the project. The unfortunate part was that the group actually knew within the first two weeks of the project that some of that critical data were not available. Instead of taking a step back, they marched forward, building out data dictionaries, data marts, and data profiles for the other less-important data elements. After six months, they found themselves with nothing to show to their business customer besides documentation.

As the team starts on its analytic project, the first step is to identify the necessary data sources. A high-level data inventory will include a list of potential data sources; data dictionaries, if available; an associated subject matter expert; and the access route. As part of the data identification process, as best as you can, classify it into two components: need-to-have and nice-to-have.

Your business and IT partners are critical in this process. In project after project, we've seen data access issues drag down the timelines of major analytic initiatives. The same applies to external data: Your data provider may need significant lead-time to turn around data requests. An emerging area of importance is data access and security. With data breaches becoming more common, organizations are putting a lot more governance and control around how data are not only accessed but used. Some industries are also subject to strict regulatory control over certain data elements. All these governance processes will impact the timeline of your project, so be sure your analytic team knows who to coordinate with.

THE DATA SPIKE

Working with the call center, Rebecca and Isabel identify the subject matter experts who will help them identify relevant data sources. They schedule a half-day brainstorming session with the group.

> Isabel begins: "When we try and understand what drives our customers to leave, there are several areas of data that we like to look at across six categories." She draws six boxes on the whiteboard (see Figure 11.2). "At this point,

Figure 11.2 Common Data Subject Areas for Customer Analytics

we just want to start inventorying what data sources are available, who is the business owner for that data, and who can help us extract the data.

"The attributes tell us who this person is. This type of information includes demographic and other profile information. We have some third-party data sources with this information, but our own first-party data will likely be more predictive.

"Then we want to try to determine what our customers' needs and values are. What's important to them? We may not have access to a lot of this information, but it's worth asking about. Do we have any surveys that capture customer satisfaction, brand perception or loyalty, or customer preferences?

"Purchase history is next. What do our customers buy? What types of products and services are they buying, and when? Do they only buy when we give them a discount?

"Interactions cover a customer's interaction history with us. This can include all different types of transactions and interactions a customer may have. Are they contacting us? How many times?

"Where customers have that interaction is very important as part of their decision-making process. What channels do they prefer? What is their online versus offline behavior?

"Finally, what competitive information do we capture? What alternatives do our customers have? This may include qualitative sources of information from market research, competitor data, and market research information.

In the discovery workshop, the team identified all data subject areas aligned to these categories. Remember that in the brainstorming session, we are not performing any detailed data or feasibility assessment, but just identifying areas of relevance and their relationships to each other. Figure 11.3 provides a high-level example of what the team created on the whiteboard. Once the team identified the subject areas, a more detailed discussion ensued on where the data lived, how the information was categorized within the company, who was the business subject matter expert (SME), and any known quality issues. In this example, after the brainstorming session, the team determined that mass media and third-party data would be out of scope for the first iteration of the project due to availability and inability to tie it back to a unique customer ID. Another benefit of creating a diagram like Figure 11.3 is that it keeps people focused.

Once the data areas had been determined, the team charged each business subject matter expert with working with his or her IT part to extract the data and make it available on an agreed on "landing zone" for further exploratory analysis. The landing zone is typically a sandbox within a database environment, or even something as simple as a set of flat files stored on a server or PC.

DATA GATHERING

The data gathering stage is all about getting access to the data and understanding it. Working with data requires knowledge of various sources of data, the systems they reside in, and any associated database platforms. Since data can come from any number of sources and be structured in any number of ways, navigating through this complexity requires a variety of skills and technical capabilities.

Depending on the structure of the analytic team and the team's engagement model (or lack of one) within the organization, the data scientist might have to perform all of the extraction and assessment work without assistance. Some will need help from their IT partners or other dedicated data resources to acquire and assess the data.

Isabel sits down with each of the data owners. "Our first step is to get a good understanding of the data. Let's start with these questions." She made the following list:

- How many years of data are available?
- What level of granularity do we have?

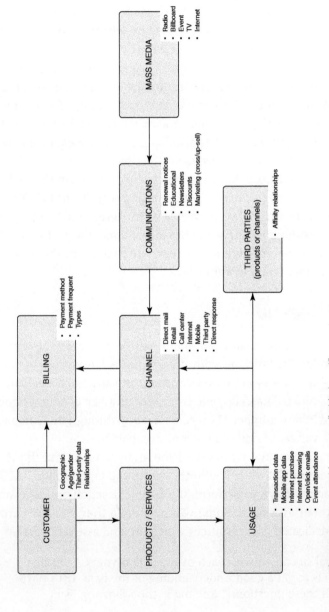

Figure 11.3 Data Subject Areas "Whiteboard"

- Is it transactional?
- Is it historical or are records overwritten—for example, customer's most current address?
- How many fields are available in the data source?
- How does the business collect and use the data?
- How are the fields related to each other?
- What is the history on the file—transformed/merged?
- Is it raw data?
- What is generating the data?
- Who uses the data?
- What data sets are created downstream?
- Is it production data?
- Is it snapshot data (as of a specific point-in-time)?
- What reports are available to validate data extracts?

If at all possible, collect a data dictionary for each available source of data. The data dictionary provides written context about the data, and can include information such as the fields in a table, the meaning of the data, and relationship to other data. The data dictionary may also include information about the table and the number of records. It's a helpful as a reference once the modeler gets deeper into each data source. While it sounds fancy, most organizations keep their data dictionaries in spreadsheets or ad-hoc databases in varying degrees of completeness. Some organizations have more formal mechanisms for capturing metadata as part of their IT processes (although this information tends to provide more technical as opposed to business context). Regardless, it would be extremely unusual to find complete data dictionaries for all data sources within an organization (Figure 11.4).

As a best practice, the modeler doesn't want direct access to source systems to pull, but will generally want to look at the most granular data possible—preferably raw data. IT resources would be required for this. IT may often offer up data that has been transformed for different purposes (such as management reporting). Try and avoid data that's been pre-transformed: Valuable data may have already been lost. If at all possible, try not to limit yourself to particular fields in the data: You'll often find hidden gems where you least expect them.

Table Description

CALL_HISTORY_TABLE

This table archives each of the call types associated with the Call History Table. This table is considered the master table for archiving all of the historical customer call center data back to January 1, 2000. The primary keys on this table is the call ID, call date and call number. To search the table for specific call types, add a constraint for Call Source on your query.

Column Name	Description	Column Type	Additional Information	Column Length	Column Order	Known Values
CALL_TRANS_ID	The unique transaction ID for each call into the call center.	varchar	With the CUST_CALL_DT, the CALL_TRANS_ID represents a unique call record.	4	1	Unique to call ID
CUSTOMER_ID	The customer ID associated with the call transaction.	varchar	The CUSTOMER_ID is tied to the CUSTOMER_MASTER_TABLE.	10	2	Unique to customer
CUST_CALL_DT	The date/time stamp for the customer call.	date time	With the CUST_CALL_DT, the CALL_TRANS_ID represents a unique call record.	12	3	Date range: 1/1/2000 to present

Figure 11.4 Data Dictionary Example

134

Using external data often requires working with data vendors who may provide files in a variety of formats. It is important for the modeler to understand these formats to identify ways to integrate the data into other internal sources.

As we mentioned, don't forget about data security and privacy: A lot of forethought must go into deciding what data will be used. In some industries, certain data fields cannot be used for some types of modeling projects. You'll also want to make sure that you adhere to any internal and external security policies around personally identifiable data. If possible, have your IT department remove or replace any confidential or restricted data prior to the data exploration phase.

VISUALIZATION AND ITERATIONS

Once the files are loaded onto the data landing area, the analytic team can begin to slice-and-dice the data. This isn't an activity that happens in isolation. Business data subject matter experts help the analyst interpret what they're seeing and understand the broader business context of the data. In fact, this is an activity that business and data analysts can participate in. The team does also not have to wait until all of the data is available to begin the analysis work.

Roughly 80 percent of your project work effort will be spent on data preparation and exploration, but it is an iterative process. The first step after data acquisition is to profile the data. This can be accomplished by running frequencies on categorical variables, histograms, or statistical analysis (mean, median, min, and max) on numeric variables. This gives the modeler an appreciation and understanding of the data quality and completeness. The reports generated from this activity provide a great starting point for additional discussions with the entire project team on the appropriateness of the data and how it should be interpreted.

> "Well," Isabel says, looking at the analysis from the available data, "it's not ideal, but I think we've got a good starting point. I've flagged the highest priority data sources and then tagged others as nice-to-have. If we can get those, great, but working with what we have today should give us some good outcomes. We can always add in new data sources down the road."

DEFINING YOUR TARGET VARIABLE

Target variable definition is the most important part of your modeling project. What are you trying to predict? If your target is time-bound (i.e., are you trying to predict a certain outcome happens within a window of time after a triggering event), how do we define the hold-out period? Are you looking to predict what happens in a 30-, 60-, or 90-day window after the event? What outcomes does the data potentially support?

You might be surprised how many people don't spend enough time clarifying their target variable and ensuring that their business partners understand it. As an example, one company was trying to predict which customers would liquidate their financial accounts after a multiyear penalty period had expired. The original goal was to identify which customers liquidated within 30 days. However, the target event (account liquidation) didn't happen with enough frequency in that time window relative to the entire population. To find a population large enough to model against, the analysts had to extend the time period to 90 days post-liquidation. Most analytic problems are not as simple as, "Yes, somebody did something," or, "No, they didn't," and let's predict why.

Again, this entire process is entirely dependent on the analytic problem you're solving and the frequency of which the event occurs in your data. There's a lot of analysis and back-and-forth that goes into this process. It's absolutely critical that your business customers understand what the approach is and have input into it.

Target variables can take the form of categorical or continuous variables. Categorical variables in modeling are more common and fall into three categories:

Dichotomous Dichotomous variables (or binary) only contain two categories or levels. In our retention project, we could have a binary target that flagged a customer as (1) retained and (0) not retained.

Nominal Nominal variables will have more than two levels, but the levels don't have an order to them. In the retention project, a customer might have different retention flags, depending on how the business interprets retention. For example, we might have several different retention scenarios: (1) customer stopped purchasing; (2) customer stopped purchasing product X; (3) customer stopped purchasing product Y.

Ordinal Ordinal variables are categorical, but have a defined sequence or rank. A Likert scale used in surveys is a good example of this (I like product X; product X is okay; I hate product X).

Analytic problems are also timebound. For example, consider our retention example—we've already established that a "lost" customer is someone that hasn't bought any products from us in six months—but that six-month window will be different for every customer. You might want to pull three to five years of data to look at the event's occurrence over time.

Yet another consideration is identifying possible outcome scenarios. In our retention example, a simple target could be: (1) yes, the customer bought something in a six-month period; or (2) no, the customer didn't buy anything. This is an example of a business rule that the organization might have in defining whether this customer is "lost" to them or not. This provides a good starting point for the first iteration of model development, but as the team gets deeper into the project, it might redefine that target based on new information. However, you might find that there are multiple outcomes that you want to model (or not). In an analytic project at one organization, what everyone thought would be a simple yes/no target turned into six possible scenarios.

Regardless, it's critical to document your assumptions and make sure the entire project team (business, IT, and analytic stakeholders) has a shared understanding of the target. We've seen more than one project fail because the analytic team made assumptions that didn't align with business expectations or understanding. Don't let this be the reason that your project fails.

> Meanwhile, Rebecca is drafting out a one-page project feasibility report for the steering committee. Based on Isabel's analysis of the customer purchase history, she's determined that the project should include two separate predictive models for retention in the first model iteration: One for customers who hadn't bought anything in six

months, but then came back and made a purchase after that, and those customers that made a purchase and then never came back.

Rebecca updates the vision statement. "Alright," she says, "let's see if we can figure out what the financial impact would be if we create models that can be used to influence customer retention."

All models are built on historical data: This makes them time-sensitive and gives them a shelf life. If the environment changes radically, then your model may no longer be relevant. Also, successful treatments—things that the organization does to influence particular outcomes—will change customer behavior, requiring a reevaluation of the model and its predictability. Considering the speed of change nature in your external business environment is also important: Business conditions continually change and you will find that the current or future state never looks exactly like the past, but should be similar enough to make valid predictions. All of these factors influence the amount of historical data used in the modeling process.

An additional challenge relates to the quantity of the data: Having a lot of records improves the quality of the prediction. There are different methodologies to handle small data sets, but when you start getting down to a few thousand records, you quickly run out of records to populate all the segments. For example, say you have 2,000 records and you have five independent variables. To make it simple, each variable is binary (yes or no). You end up with 32 possible segmentations. If the records were miraculously spread evenly among the 32 segments, each segment would have 62 records. If the data is split 70 percent/30 percent between a modeling data set and validation data set, each segment in the validation would have 19 records. This is not enough data to base a decision on.

SUMMARY

In most analytic projects, expect that the majority of your team's time will be spent on data collection and analysis, but it is an ongoing, iterative process. Short, timeboxed data spikes prior to beginning the project help ground the team in what information will be available, who owns it, and how you'll work with it moving forward. Guide your team through a data brainstorming exercise, to inventory all the available data sources and begin some initial profiling of the data to better understand the quality and completeness of it. As you define your target variable, ensure that your business partners understand the logic behind your decision-making processes.

CHAPTER 12

Shaping the Analytic Product Backlog

gile teams don't compile a large inventory of requirements up front, but instead create placeholders for requirements—our user stories—that form the backbone of the product backlog. Each product backlog item represents some component of business value. Initially, the backlog items may be very large in scope with little detail associated with them. As the backlog is prioritized, the stakeholders, product owner, and development team refine and clarify them into a collection of smaller backlog items. When backlog items are small and detailed enough, they can be moved into a sprint (see Figure 12.1). Not all requirements are at the same level of detail at the same time: A strategy of progressive refinement (or elaboration) is used to decompose large, lightly detailed requirements into smaller, more detailed components as they are slotted for analytic development work.

CREATING YOUR ANALYTIC PRODUCT BACKLOG

Most backlogs are made up of user stories that have tangible value to the customer, but may also include data defects, technical improvements, or knowledge-based work, as shown in Table 12.1.

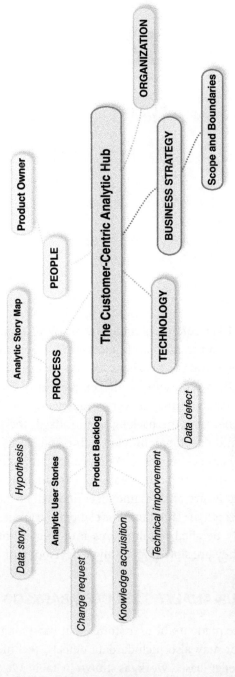

Figure 12.1 Analytic Product Backlog Considerations

Table 12.1 Analytic Product Backlog Items

Backlog Item Type	Description
Hypothesis	A feature is something that provides value or meaning to the end-customer; typically expressed as a user story—the features in our analytic project can encompass hypotheses or actual outputs of the project (e.g., propensity scores).
Data Story	A particular data element or attribute that needs to be collected and analyzed.
Change	A request to change existing end-user functionality; could include usability and design of model.
Data defect	Defects in data.
Technical improvement	Software, hardware, or DBMS upgrades needed for the project.
Knowledge acquisition	Data discovery and exploration, prototypes, architectural spikes.

In Chapter 9, "Gathering Analytic User Stories," the team created a number of user stories in the form of hypotheses at the story workshop. These stories form the backbone of the product backlog. It's the product owner's responsibility to assist the team in prioritizing the backlog. Throughout the project duration, the user stories will be more fully fleshed out by the project team and slotted to an iteration or sprint during the planning process. The product owner can change the priority of the stories as long as the story isn't in development.

If the project is very large or if there are a lot of dependencies or complex details, product backlog items might be captured in the form of a product roadmap. The product roadmap is an artifact used in the planning process that anticipates how the analysis and analytic deliverables will shape over time. This planning document helps cement the shared vision of the product across the different stakeholder groups, including the product owner and the project team. Additionally, the roadmap facilitates coordination between and across project streams by providing a high-level view of the project, its capabilities and target customers. The roadmap's planning horizon generally looks out no longer than 6 to 12 months.

Another approach used by project teams is the story map popularized by Jeff Patton (2008) to help select and group capabilities by release cycle. The story map is comprised of three areas:

The Backbone The backbone reflects essential functionality that needs to be performed by the system. This functionality is not optional and therefore should not be prioritized. This could include data or other technology infrastructure considerations.

Walking Skeleton The walking skeleton contains minimally required capabilities that are essential to the project.

Capabilities Capabilities represent functionality that can be prioritized based on importance.

The team orders the story map by importance and sequence and defines releases based on the amount of insight that the team believes it can deliver within a certain time frame. Figure 12.2 illustrates the structure of the story map. A simple way to think about organizing a story map is by defining the workflow—story themes can be placed along a timeline based on a sequence of events. For example, in our retention project, source data analysis will come before any segmentation work, or we may sequence the work by different data source layers. Story mapping can be done after a story workshop to help group and prioritize user stories.

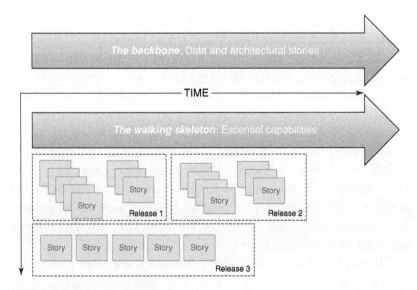

Figure 12.2 The Analytic Story Map

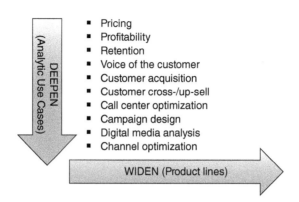

Figure 12.3 Analytic Story Backbone: Customer Analytic Program

For one organization, they identified user story categories and created an iterative strategy for going both deep into the categories and wide across the types of analysis needed within a single category across product families (see Figure 12.3).

GOING DEEP

A widely used practice for managing the product backlog is to go DEEP (Pichler, 2010). The DEEP acronym stands for: detailed appropriately, emergent, estimated, and prioritized. Using the DEEP criteria can help determine if the backlog is structured appropriately.

> *Detailed Appropriately* High-priority items contain more details than low-priority items. This ensures that too much data is not collected upfront and the team is focused on the top items in the queue. The highest-priority product backlog items should be small and detailed enough to include in the next sprint. As the team reaches down into the queue, large backlog items (often still "epics" at this point) are refined in a just-in-time manner. This is a careful balance: If the item is refined too early, the team may be wasting time on something that isn't important; and if they refine too late, it may drag down a sprint.
>
> *Emergent* The product backlog is continually updated based on new information provided by internal and external stakeholders. As a

result, the product backlog emerges over time. The product owner takes all of these inputs and uses it to rebalance and reprioritize items within the product backlog.

Estimated Each backlog item has a development size estimate associated with it. If a large item makes it to the top of the backlog, that is an indicator to the team that refinement must take place before it can be moved into a sprint. Estimates are often based in story points or ideal days, which will be covered in our next chapter.

Prioritized More likely than not, only near-term backlog items are going to be prioritized—perhaps through a release cycle. Since the product owner is constantly taking in new information, the priority of items shifts based on customer input, organizational priorities and competitive or market influences.

PRODUCT BACKLOG GROOMING

Grooming is the process of managing, organizing, and administrating the product backlog. There are three principal activities in the grooming process: creating and refining, estimating, and prioritizing product backlog items. Grooming is a constant activity throughout the project duration. While the product owner retains primary responsibility (and is the decision maker) for prioritizing and grooming, it is a collaborative process.

While customers write the initial requirements, the analytic Scrum team begins to contribute to the story as the details are refined. Grooming may take place at any time—some teams may groom each day after their daily standup meetings; others may do a deeper dive on it weekly, or even wait until the end of a sprint. Regardless of the frequency, the analytic Scrum team should get into the habit of grooming on a consistent basis. A well-groomed backlog is a necessity for planning an iteration or sprint (see Figure 12.4).

DEFINING "READY"

Before moving product backlog items into a sprint cycle, the analytic Scrum team may require that the items meet the definition of *ready*. Coupled with the definition of *done* (which we'll review in our

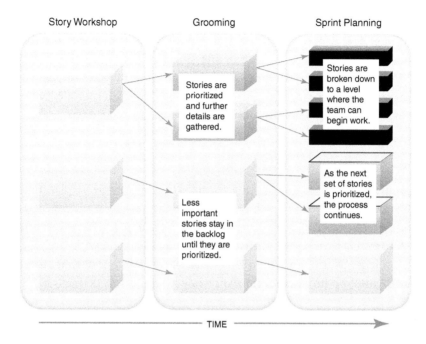

Figure 12.4 The Product Backlog Evolves Over Time

Chapter 13), readiness defines the state of the backlog items prior to a sprint cycle. By ensuring that the items are ready to be worked on, the analysts will have greater confidence in their ability to complete the work during the sprint. The readiness checklist is defined by the team and may include requirements such as the following:

- Clear articulation of business value.
- Sufficient understanding of details and data sources.
- Identified dependencies across the stories.
- Estimated and sized appropriately for the sprint.
- Hypothesis acceptance criteria can be validated.
- Demonstrable analysis, visualization, profiles, or results.

MANAGING FLOW

The concept of flow is one of the key principles of agile, with roots in the lean process improvement methodology. The goal of flow is to keep an item moving smoothly through a process or workstream without delays or roadblocks. Maintaining flow is important across your project through the release and sprint cycles in creating a predictable and sustainable flow of work. One of the biggest challenges that analytic teams face is managing the flow of work, especially when provisioning, understanding, and exploring data.

Release Flow Management

A well-groomed product backlog supports the flow of release planning. One recommended approach is to prioritize the backlog into three categories: must-have, nice-to-have, and won't-have. Must-haves fall into the current release; nice-to-haves can either be included in the current release or the next one (if the team is running out of time, these items could be dropped); and won't-haves would not be included in the release. The prioritization method keeps the release flow moving, since it is clear which items are important within a release cycle. This technique can really help teams that are struggling with problem data sources. As with stories, data can also be categorized as must-have or nice-to-have.

Sprint Flow Management

Consistent grooming helps ensure that the product backlog items are appropriately detailed and estimated for slotting into a sprint. This creates a flow of stories for each sprint. As requirements move through the pipeline, they are progressively prioritized, decomposed, and estimated until they are ready for inclusion within a sprint.

When the inflow and outflow of backlog items is mismatched, then flow is disrupted. For example, if the team hasn't groomed enough items, it might start a sprint planning cycle without enough detailed requirements to select for the sprint. If there are too many fully groomed items in the pipeline that the team can't complete in a single sprint, then the grooming effort spent on the extra items may go to waste.

As a rule of thumb, many Scrum teams keep around two to three sprints worth of work ready to go. So if the team can complete five items in a given sprint, then it might have 10 to 15 lined up. Having just the right amount of extra inventory allows the team to select additional items, if it has capacity, and provides buffer in the pipeline.

The XP methodology provides similar guidance on iteration and release planning by planning at the last responsible moment (Shore and Warden, 2008). The last responsible moment is the latest point in time at which you can responsibly make a decision. The further out an event, the less detail will be contained in your plan. It's recommended that you use tiered planning horizons, where long planning horizons are used for general plans and short planning horizons are used for detailed plans. As a rule, the more commitments that are made to stakeholders, the longer the planning horizon should be. If the situation is uncertain, or new information is likely to change the plan, use a shorter planning horizon.

SUMMARY

Product planning activities generate a list of user stories or requirements captured as the product backlog. The prioritized high-level product backlog is organized into a series of planned releases, often in the form of a product roadmap. The product backlog provides the backbone of the Scrum framework. This list of desired features and functionality of the system is groomed continually throughout the project, according to DEEP principles. The grooming process is a continuous activity performed by the team throughout the project. Before backlog items are moved into a sprint, they should meet the team's definition of ready. The team needs to keep a just-in-time inventory of analytic items ready for sprint planning to ensure sprint flow.

CHAPTER **13**

The Analytic Sprint: Planning and Execution

I n our previous chapters, we've covered processes and activities within the Scrum framework. In this chapter, our analytic team gets rolling on its project with sprint planning activities. Team members timebox their sprint planning session at two hours and use the time to review roles and responsibilities, define a sprint goal, and select backlog items that they believe they can complete during the sprint, based on their velocity. The team incorporates a definition of done into the task estimation to ensure high-quality, customer-ready deliverables (see Figure 13.1).

COMMITTING THE TEAM

In Chapter 8 on analytic Scrum roles and responsibilities, we discussed three roles: the product owner, ScrumMaster, and development team, which can comprise any roles necessary to complete the work. In addition, you may identify a few extra roles that are important, whether related to organizational requirements or specific project needs. There's no one "right" team structure: As long as you have access to all of the

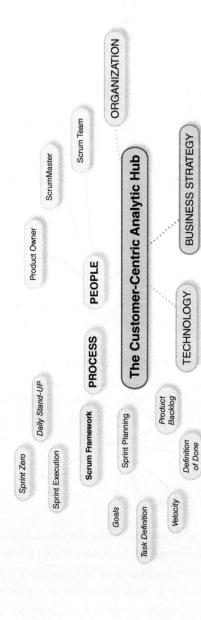

Figure 13.1 The Product Backlog Evolves over Time

knowledge that's required to get the work done, you can organize in whatever way makes sense.

> Rebecca and Isabel review all of their planning documents. "We've got Sherry as our sponsor and Jason as our day-to-day product owner. Sherry's there to assist with any data preparation work and Sally as our dedicated IT liaison. Jeremy and Natasha will be doing the modeling work. I'll be the team's ScrumMaster, and I'd like to bring in Emily, one of our business analysts, to help the modelers with the documentation. That should do it for our full-time team. On an as-needed basis, we'll bring in the data SMEs. Since we're starting with the customer data, Jason will be working with us full-time for the next two sprints."

Ideally, the core team is dedicated full-time to the project. With roles such as our data SME, whose expertise is only required for a specific component of the project, they don't have to be with the team for the duration. However, during the time that they're needed, they should be fully allocated and available.

THE PLAYERS

Table 13.1 is an overview of our team members, their roles, and a description of their responsibilities. Note that this is just a list of team members and is not reflective of all the stakeholders in the project. While Isabel leads the analytic team, she won't play an active role in the execution of the work.

A key tenet of Scrum is that the Scrum team is self-organizing. This means that the team determines who the work will be assigned to within the team and how it will be completed. As outputs of the sprint planning process, the Scrum team knows what the sprint goal is and what backlog items will be delivered during sprint execution. Also within sprint planning, the team creates a plan for completing product backlog items assigned to the sprint. This effort does not involve creating a detailed project plan or Gantt chart for the sprint. Scrum is designed to let teams learn by doing, and this learning process is disruptive to detailed planning. That said, a level of up-front planning is

Table 13.1 The Players

Person	Role	Description
Jim Allen, AVP of Customer Service	Product Owner	Jim will provide the day-to-day guidance on the direction of the project, including the prioritization of the team's product backlog.
Rebecca Gonzales, Project Lead, Analytics	ScrumMaster	Rebecca's role is the ScrumMaster. She'll ensure that the team has everything they need to be successful.
Natasha Stoykova, Lead Data Scientist, Analytics	Development Team Member	Natasha is the most experienced analyst on the team and provides analytic coaching to other team members.
Jeremy Liu, Jr. Data Scientist, Analytics	Development Team Member	Jeremy will work closely with Natasha to complete the analytic work.
Sarah Martin, ETL Specialist, Analytics	Development Team Member	While Sarah's specialty is ETL and data integration, she has profiling and basic statistical skills.
Sally Martinez, IT Operations	Development Team Member	Sally is primarily the IT liaison, but also supports the data environment and can help with data extraction and profiling tasks.
Emily O'Brien, Business Analyst, Analytics	Business Analyst	Emily assists the team in completing the definition of done, by helping to capture the knowledge gained during the analysis and formulating the reports and visualization needed in the sprint review.
Jason Chu, Director of Customer Service	Data Subject Matter Expert, Customer Data	Since the focus of this sprint is on customer data, Jason will assist the team in selecting the right data elements and interpreting their business context.

helpful in identifying task-level dependencies, but should be limited to the knowledge the team has at hand. Teams that apply task planning continuously during the sprint will assist them in adapting to change.

SPRINT PLANNING

Rebecca assembles the team for its first two-hour sprint planning meeting. Isabel and Sherry are conspicuously absent.

"Hey, where's Isabel?" asks Jim. "I thought she would be here?"

"Isabel participates in the prioritization and upfront planning that we do prior to project execution, but once a project gets rolling, the team takes over," says Rebecca. "Since this is the first planning meeting we're having as a team, let's go over some of the ground rules and expectations. In our meeting last week, we groomed our product backlog and identified our first area of focus—the customer data in our CDW. Our first step is to define the sprint goal."

"Remind me again," says Jim, "what's a sprint goal?"

"The sprint goal gives our Scrum team a target for our first sprint. As the product owner, you get to define that goal, keeping in mind the work that's on the backlog and our capacity—or velocity, the amount of work the team believes they can complete in a sprint—to complete the work within our one-week sprint time frame."

VELOCITY

Teams measure the amount of work completed in a sprint by calculating their velocity. Velocity is calculated by adding up the size of the product backlog items completed at the sprint's finish. Partially completed product backlog items do not count in a team's velocity metric. Velocity measures the team's output, not the value of the output.

A team's velocity plays a critical role in Scrum planning processes. At the release-level, the team adds up the total story points within a release and then divides that by the team's average velocity to come up with the number of sprints within the release. Velocity is also used as an input for evaluating and improving the team's processes. By reviewing velocity over time, the team can analyze the impact of process changes on its ability to deliver customer value.

If your team is brand new or the type of project you're delivering is new, you won't have any historical velocity metrics to use during the planning process. In that case, the team needs to forecast velocity. One method would be to have the team plan out a sprint and estimate the number of product backlog items that the team believes could be completed during the sprint. For the release plan, that estimated velocity could be used in place of average velocity. Once a sprint has been completed and the team has an actual velocity measure, the team can re-estimate the release plan.

> "Since this is a new project, we took a stab at calculating velocity for our first sprint," Rebecca tells the team. "We have five development team members. Our sprint one work will be heavily weighted toward data extraction and profiling, but the entire team has the skillset to participate in those activities. On a typical project, we use a 32-hour workweek. This helps us account for any administrative time and other meetings that take place throughout the week. If we multiply 5 development team members by 32 hours per week, we have 160 person-hours per sprint. Working from our product backlog and aligning to the sprint goal, we'll tackle that amount of work in our sprint.

> "What we might find down the road," she continues, "is that we have more capacity, or we have opportunities to improve our estimation. All those things will go into future sprint planning sessions. But this gives us a good starting point."

TASK DEFINITION

The team decides what tasks need to be accomplished to complete a product backlog item. While managers and product owners may provide input into task-level work (by defining the scope of the feature and the acceptance criteria), they must trust and empower the team to define and organize the completion of that work.

The nature of the business requirements may also influence how the work is completed. For example, if the team needs to deliver customer-ready work in a production environment, there may be more work effort involved for customer-readiness. If specific technical decisions are made that have business and/or financial consequences, they need to be taken into account in a way that makes sense for the business. These types of requirements would be included in the team's definition of done.

Teams should decompose stories into tasks that can be completed in a few hours. The definition of tasks at a granular level helps enforce discipline to develop and deliver small increments of functionality.

Rebecca hands out the current product backlog that the team worked on in its initial grooming session, shown in Table 13.2.

> "Perfect," says Jim. "I want the first sprint goal to be this: Identify available customer attributes that could influence retention."
>
> "That's a great start," says Rebecca, "but the team needs to ensure that they can complete all of these tasks within the sprint. Team, what do you think?"
>
> "I think it's reasonable," Natasha looks over the task list. "We went over this while we were grooming. This totals up to 107 ideal hours. We believe our velocity is 160 hours. I think this is a good starting point since this is our first sprint. If we find that we have excess capacity, we can take on additional work, but we absolutely don't want to take on more work than we know we can finish."

The team agrees on the sprint goal and begins to decompose some of the tasks in the backlog. As a general rule, tasks longer than eight ideal hours in duration (the amount of time a task would take

Table 13.2 Analytic Sprint Tasks

Hypothesis	Data Source	Data Tables	Data Stories	Tasks
Customer attributes influence retention	CDW External customer demo-graphic	Table 1 Table 2 Table 3 Table 4	How old are customers? Where do they live? What is their income?	Extract customer data from CDW (5 hours) Create master customer file (16 hours) Extract and merge external data with customer data (20 hours) Land data in analytic sandbox (2 hours) Profile and assess data (24 hours) Perform cluster analysis (8 hours) Complete data assessment report (8 hours) Document data sources (24 hours)

without interruptions) should be broken down into more discrete tasks. For example, the task labeled "create master customer file" might be broken down into tasks like:

- Take customer attribute table and append to customer table.
- Aggregate data by household.
- Append additional customer tables.

Cohn (2004) recommends the following guidelines for task decomposition:

- If one task of a story is difficult to estimate, separate the task from the rest of the story.
- If tasks can be easily completed by separate developers, then split those tasks.
- If there is benefit in knowing that part of a story is complete, then break that part out as a separate task.

THE TEAM'S DEFINITION OF DONE

The purpose behind creating the definition of done (DOD) is to ensure that the team delivered completed work to its customers. All too often, teams take shortcuts to get the work out the door: A solid DOD helps the team deliver high-quality results to stakeholders and minimizes technical debt. DOD tasks are included as part of the team's estimates. Following are examples of tasks for the team to consider—some of these may be encompassed in the definition of done and would be incorporated in every data story or hypothesis the team is working on. Keep in mind that you don't have to go overboard on this—your team should create a DOD list that makes sense for the organization and adds value to your stakeholders (including your team!).

Story elements: Tasks for any additional whiteboarding or discussion needed around hypothesis or data story clarification.

Code checks: Create a task for validating model dataset ETL or other code.

Nonfunctional requirements: Tasks to account for any security, performance, usability, testability, maintainability, extensibility, scalability, and regulatory needs; these tasks become more important as the predictive models move out of development and into operational deployment.

Peer review: Peer review of analytic methodology, assumptions, results, coding, ETL, and so on.

Code refactoring: Tasks for restructuring of model development code in an efficient manner; again, a task like this may be more critical to production deployment of a model. For example, an ETL developer may refactor an analyst's data preparation or integration code to conform to production standards.

Exploratory testing: Ad hoc testing to ensure nonfunctional requirements specifications have been met.

Data defects verification and fix: Allocating the appropriate time for validation and verification of analysis or results prior to sharing it with stakeholders.

Documentation: Tasks for updating any data dictionary or knowledge repository with the appropriate documentation (data profiling results, data sources and definitions, statistical analyses, etc.).

End-user documentation: Tasks for creating any materials (reports or visualizations) used to communicate findings to stakeholders.

Your DOD may be project specific, team specific, or a combination of both. For any strategic project, Isabel's team uses a DOD that starts with specific team requirements and layers in any additional requirements required by either IT or the business stakeholders. For example, if the team is working on a project that uses confidential data, the team adds in criteria to align organizational data security standards.

ORGANIZING WORK

Most simply, the team may select the highest- priority items to work on as defined during the sprint planning session. This ensures that items not completed by the end of the sprint are of lower priority. However, this approach may not be realistic due to technical dependencies or skill capacity, which may force the team to complete work in a different order. This is an important consideration for the team members as they plan their work. In our project, there is some sequence to the work, meaning that there is task dependency. For example, you might not be able to start profiling until the data have landed in the sandbox. However, you might be able to start profiling individual data sets before the aggregation work is complete.

Once a backlog item has been selected, the team determines how to perform the task-level work. It's important for the team to get away from the waterfall mindset: Work can be ordered in any way that is effective for the team. The team also needs to get away from thinking about role-based work. Agile teams often share responsibilities or take on different roles during development. This minimizes idle time and reduces the number of handoffs throughout the development process. In this sprint, all of our team members have basic data profiling and analysis skills, so that work could be shared.

Once the tasks have been identified, team members will typically volunteer to perform a task. The team member responsible for the task records his or her name next to the task (perhaps on a whiteboard or within an agile software management tool). Even if using pair-programming during development, one person should accept responsibility for task completion. But it's important to keep in mind that the team is in this together: The group shares responsibility for ensuring that everything is completed.

SPRINT ZERO

Although it might sound counterintuitive since there's no customer value in it, the team may initiate a sprint zero before beginning to work on development tasks. Within sprint zero, team members focus on getting things ready for the development process so they can hit the ground running in their first sprint. This could include developing the release plan and backlog, infrastructure set-up, and architectural design considerations, and establishing team practices and standards. Many Scrum practitioners advocate against a sprint zero, but it may be appropriate for the team if some of the following conditions are in place:

New Teams The team may need some time to organize and discuss how it will work together. For new analytic projects, engaging IT and the business and developing those relationships will take some time.

New Infrastructure, Tools, or Methods If the team doesn't have any experience with a certain programming language, software application, hardware configuration, database environment, and so on, you can use this time for training or level setting.

Geographic Distribution or Cross-Team Work Efforts Use this opportunity to ensure that the team's communication/collaboration tools are working well and that the environment works from different geographic locations.

Sprint zero is not required, but may be useful for teams that are just getting started. As with any sprint, the team should define a sprint goal to work toward. A successful sprint zero enables the team to begin development quickly in sprint one. Keep your sprint zero timeboxed so you don't end up in an infinite no-customer-value analysis phase.

Often, in a new analytic project, the team may be testing a new technology or capability. If there is a dependency in your project on one of these capabilities, make sure you have the tools in place to begin the work in your sprint. It's absolutely appropriate to layer in technology capabilities over time, but you want the minimum infrastructure in place day one to get started. If your team needs training on some new capability within the duration of your project, carve out the time in a knowledge-gathering spike.

> Sally reviews the product backlog. "The big data infrastructure we're putting up in Hadoop won't be ready for a couple of weeks. We'll need to defer any data stories related to web data until that's in place. I'll continue to work with that team so we're kept in the loop."

SPRINT EXECUTION

> Once the foundation has been laid, the team begins its work. The data begin to roll into the analytic sandbox, and the team members begin their profiling work. At the team's daily standup on day three of the sprint, it's Natasha's turn to speak.

"Since yesterday, I've been working on profiling our customer data sources. I'm going to continue the profiling work today, but we've got some issues with the data that need to be addressed before we can move forward."

"Can you give me a quick overview?" says Rebecca.

Natasha continues, "As we were preparing the data, we discovered that many of the data fields were never entered with the understanding that it would be used for analysis. For example:

"Many fields are not required, meaning that they could be left blank, allowing for a large amount of missing values.

"Most categorical fields do not have well-defined levels. This means that at one point in time, a categorical level could be assigned a value and then a few years later, another categorical level meaning essentially the same thing could be assigned a different value. This results in a larger number of values for that category.

"There are inaccurate date values associated with birthdates and other customer expiration dates.

"Jason and I have been working through why some of this is happening and Emily is documenting it, but this is a discussion point for the broader team. We've got some ideas on how to work around this. I recommend that we continue work on the assessment during this sprint and then use our sprint review time on Friday to discuss with our customers."

"Is there anything else I can do to help you?" asks Rebecca.

"I think we're okay for now. We'll give you another update tomorrow morning."

This is a good example of why a one-week sprint works well for this analytic team. The sprint review checkpoint provides frequent enough checkpoints with the business stakeholders so that critical issues like these can be addressed. If the analytic team moves forward with its own solution without consulting the customers, then the team runs the risk of producing results that the business may not trust. This also illustrates the importance of having a dedicated product owner and data SME on the team. While these problems in our team's project are not insurmountable, it requires a conversation between the team and the stakeholders.

SUMMARY

The analytic Scrum team begins its first sprint in a sprint planning session. Once the sprint goal is defined, the team selects the appropriate amount of work that the team members reasonably believe that they can complete during the sprint. As the team initiates the project, a "sprint zero" may be helpful for preparing the environment and infrastructure. Defining tasks in accordance with the team's definition of done is critical for a successful sprint. The team self-organizes: Once tasks are defined, the team determines who will perform the work and how it will be completed. The team leverages technical development practices in performing the work through its definition of done.

CHAPTER 14

The Analytic Sprint: Review and Retrospective

After the team completes the sprint, it comes together with the broader customer group to review the completed work. During sprint execution, the team found a few problems with the customer data. While team members have some recommendations, they need to review with their customers and get feedback before they move forward. When the sprint review is over, the team meets for a short sprint retrospective that allows it to identify areas where the team did well and areas that need improvement (see Figure 14.1). Following the retrospective, the team jumps right back into planning the next sprint with the product owner.

SPRINT REVIEW

The purpose of the sprint review is to share results with your customers and get feedback. Prior to the sprint review meeting, the team makes sure that all of the results that it will share meet the team's definition of done. Some teams review work with the product owner prior to the formal review meeting. In any case, the sprint

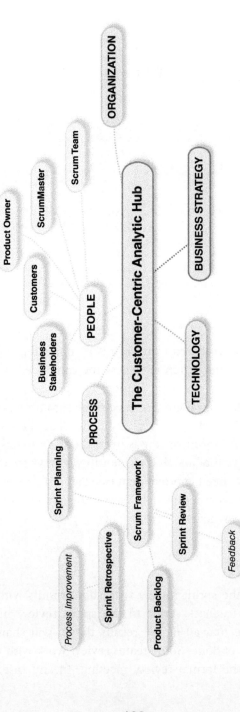

Figure 14.1 Analytic Sprint Review and Retrospective Considerations

review meeting shouldn't be the first time your product owner is see-ing results. Engaging and sharing output with your product owner throughout the sprint is important as it helps avoid surprises for both the customer and the team. But be cautious: As the product owner works with the team during the sprint, asks questions, and clarifies, the work in progress should not fundamentally change. For example, the product owner shouldn't add any work or request changes that might alter the focus of the sprint goal.

The sprint review is a low-ceremony, high-value event. That means that the sprint reviews are critical in providing feedback and direction for the project, but the team doesn't need to overprepare. Preparation for the meeting shouldn't take longer than 30 to 60 minutes. In our analytic project, preparation might include reports or analysis that the team is going to share with the customers. The team may also bring a laptop to share some data visualization—allowing customers to ask question and see results in real-time.

In the sprint, the team has uncovered some problems with the data in the customer data warehouse. Many of the customer attribute fields that the team would like to use to create the customer profile are incomplete. Working with the data SME, the team has identified a workaround. It can supplement the internal customer attributes with attributes from a third-party data set. For example, the internal field for customer age is only 50 percent complete. Missing data can be sup-plemented with data from the external file where available, but the team wants to validate that approach with the customers.

The team presents the following findings from its analysis:

- The business doesn't require that most customer attributes be filled out in its current CRM application. This resulted in a large amount of missing values. Working with the product owner and the SMEs, we determined the best approach was to exclude these variables from the analysis at this time.
- Most categorical fields (i.e., fields with a fixed set of values) do not have well-defined levels. This means that at one point in time, a categorical level could be assigned a value and then a few years later, another categorical level meaning essentially the same thing

could be assigned a different value, resulting in more or ambiguous values than expected. We connected with an expert in the call center and were able to identify a way to streamline the values.

- Many date values are inaccurate. At the point of entry, customer service reps may fill out a 1/1/1900 value for a birthdate if they can't collect the information. We were able to overlay external third-party data to supplement missing values. Our analysis shows us that age is a critical variable in the analysis.

Roles and Responsibilities

In a typical sprint review meeting, the ScrumMaster will facilitate and guide the session. The product owner gives an overview of the sprint goal and a high-level summary of the work accomplished. The team will present the results. It is recommended that each developer present his or her own work.

SPRINT RETROSPECTIVE

For those with an understanding of the traditional project management process, you might be familiar with the concept of a "lessons learned" session at the end of the project. While that can be a valuable exercise in some respects, it doesn't allow the team to improve during the project.

One of the 12 principles of The Agile Manifesto is this: *At regular intervals, the team reflects on how to become more effective, then tunes and adjusts its behavior accordingly.*

While it might be tempting for the team to skip this step—don't! The retrospective helps the team to reflect and adjust inflight, facilitating the improvement of its productivity, capability, capacity, and quality. Although the daily standup meeting helps identify barriers and bottlenecks, the retrospective is designed to help the team improve processes, engagement, and environment.

Like other Scrum ceremonies, the retrospective is timeboxed, typically around 30 minutes. This keeps the team focused. Don't feel like you have to fill up the time if the team doesn't have a lot to review in a sprint. Since our analytic team's sprints are so short, team members generally find that 15 minutes is plenty of time to cover the relevant topics. If your sprints are running in two- to four-week increments, you'll likely need the extra time.

Team members or even external parties (like an agile coach) can facilitate a retrospective meeting. In fact, many teams find it beneficial to rotate facilitators to encourage engagement and participation. Depending on how your sprint has progressed, the team may even define a particular objective for the retrospective (focusing on quality issues or technical practices). Remember that the only attendees at the retrospective are the Scrum team: product owner, ScrumMaster, and development team.

Teams should also establish meeting ground rules. As Isabel and Rebecca were working on creating the analytic Scrum methodology for their team, they drafted meeting guidelines and reviewed with the analytic team. First and foremost, they wanted to ensure that participants felt safe during the meeting: They wanted to create an environment where people felt comfortable speaking their mind and engaging in constructive discussion and even conflict.

> After the sprint review, the team heads back to the war room for a 30-minute retrospective. The execution of the first sprint went pretty well, with the exception of some of the data quality issues. At the sprint review meeting, some of the business stakeholders were upset that the quality issues weren't brought to them as they were uncovered. The team decides that the focus for its retrospective will be around customer engagement.
>
> Jeremy is facilitating the session. He goes to the whiteboard and writes the retrospective agenda down:
>
> - Focus area: Improve customer engagement
> - Agenda items:
> - Team check-in
> - How do we think we did on a scale of 1-5?
> - What inhibitors got in the way of achieving this objective?

- What can we improve?
- Do we need anyone else's help to achieve our goal?
- Next steps and action items

Jeremy does a quick round-table and checks in with each team member. "I just want to get the pulse of the team. I know we're focusing on customer engagement in this retrospective, but how's everything else going?" Each person speaks in turn; no additional concerns are voiced at this time.

"Great," he says, "I think we've definitely started our project off strong as a team. Based on the review meeting, our customers have said that they want to be informed more quickly when we find issues with the data."

"Well, I actually think we did a good job," said Natasha. "We decided as a team to hold off until the review meeting. I think what surprised everyone was not that we waited a couple of days, but that there were additional stakeholders that wanted the information. I would recommend reviewing the stakeholder list and communication plan."

Rebecca nods. "I agree with that. I captured the additional customers that attended our sprint review. I can draft up a new communication plan for those folks, but before I do that, we need Jim's approval since he's the product owner and customers are technically his responsibility. Jim—what do you think?"

Jim scratches his chin. "Well, I hadn't realized that their input was going to be that critical, which is why they weren't included in the first place. What I want to be cautious of is having so many people with their fingers in the pie, that we won't be able to accomplish anything. I tell you what—let me go meet with them individually, and I'll talk to Sherry. I'll get back to you on whether we should update our communication plan."

Jason speaks up: "As we were going through the data review, I didn't realize that Ramona was such an expert on our customer data. If it's all right with the team, I would like to pull her into some additional discussions. Her input could be really valuable, and it might help alleviate some of the concerns the broader stakeholder group had around communication and input."

Jeremy captures the action items. "Here's what I have—Jason will have a discussion with Sherry around the stakeholders. Is there a date that you can get back to us by?" Jim nods. "I'm meeting with her on Monday. I'll stop by after that." Jeremy continues, "And then our only other action item is including Ramona on our data discussions. Jason, will you take that?" "You bet," he says.

There's nothing worse than a retrospective meeting where there are no action items or takeaways. If people aren't acting on the information, then they'll be less likely to see value in the meeting or in contributing. Once creating action items, the team needs to hold itself accountable for the completion of those items. In our team's first retrospective, we have two follow-ups with clear accountability. Fortunately, it's early on in our project and things are easy to address. If the team identifies something in the retrospective that might require significant effort (e.g., an overhaul in the way the team tests the code), that item might need to go onto the product backlog for prioritization.

Teams on large projects may even create a retrospective backlog to improve their processes. This is a great idea as long as teams have the discipline to follow up on the backlog items. In our example, the team might find opportunities to improve its quality practices, but since the improvement effort might span outside the scope of the project, it requires a different level of attention.

Table 14.1 is a release retrospective from another analytic project.

SPRINT PLANNING (AGAIN)

After the team wraps up the retrospective session and assigns action items, the next planning session begins. Since the team is running in one-week sprints, it's better to wrap up the review, retrospective, and planning in a single afternoon. This will allow the team to hit the ground running on Monday morning. Coming out of the sprint review meeting, the team has additional items for the product backlog. Team members also have the go-ahead to use the external customer data where their own internal data are missing.

Table 14.1 Analytic Team Retrospective Example

Attributes	Overview	The Good	Needs Improvement
Empowered team	• Three full sprint cycles and a release • Team members shared roles/responsibilities • Instructor as agile coach	• Team gelled! • Settled into routine	• Communication
Customer-centric	• Product vision • User personas • User stories • Sprint themes and goals	• Understood the significance of user-centric design and development	• Estimation process • Slipped into old habits • Learning curve with agile PM tool • Dedicated product owner (instructor/facilitator)
Inspect-and-adapt	• Technical practices/testing approach • Retrospectives	• Definition of done • Retrospectives	• Identification and ownership of action items

Natasha looks over the product backlog. "I think next week we'll have enough information to start looking at transactional data and define our target variable. Jim, how do you feel about that as our next sprint goal?"

"That doesn't seem very ambitious," he says, "we already know what the target is."

"My experience tells me that there's a lot more nuances around defining the target. If we're lucky, it's a simple yes/no—the customer either did something or didn't do something. But in looking at some of the data last week, I think we have a number of different potential outcomes for customers related to retention. We'll have to identify those scenarios and confirm with the stakeholders. It's critical that we get the target right and have business sign off; otherwise, the entire modeling effort will be for nothing.

"Besides," she continues, "if it ends up being a really simple scenario, we can always take on additional work. After we get through transactional data, what's the next area of data exploration?"

"Let's move some of the product line detail up on the backlog," says Jim. "I think that will be very complimentary to the work on the transactional data. Let's start with the product line that has the most sales and work from there."

LAYERING IN COMPLEXITY

Agile is beneficial to analytic projects in that it lets the team layer in complexity over time. Instead of trying to assemble a giant dataset and creating a number of predictive models at the end of the process, the team can analyze and model the data throughout the project. Through this process, you create some natural stage-gates (in the frequency of your sprints) that allow the organization to make better, more informed decisions. These decisions could be as dramatic as determining whether to move forward with a project or not, or as simple as overcoming lapses in business understanding or determining how to overcome obstacles with data availability or quality.

During the next sprint planning meeting, the team adds a couple of data stories identified during the sprint review meeting, as shown in Table 14.2. Jim agrees that the new stories that address the missing data problem from sprint one should be incorporated into the next sprint. They are added to the backlog and the team repeats the planning process.

As the team goes through each sprint, team members uncover new information that influences the next work effort. In a project like this, there is a time element to the data that is important to consider. For example, if you define attrition as "customer hasn't bought anything from us in six months," that six-month period will be different for every customer. Structuring the data to account for the different time dimensions for each customer record can be technically challenging. Our target (or dependent) variable is "no sales in six months," and all of our independent variables need to reflect activity prior to that

Table 14.2 Analytic Data Stories

Sprint	Goal	Data Source	Data Stories	Tasks	Decision Points
#1	Identify available customer attributes	CDW External customer demo- graphic data	How old are the customers? Where do they live? What is their income?	Extract customer data from CDW (5 hours) Create master customer file (16 hours) Extract and merge external data with customer data (20 hours) Land data in analytic sandbox (2 hours) Profile and assess data (24 hours) Perform cluster analysis (8 hours) Complete data assessment report (8 hours) Document data sources (24 hours)	How do we handle missing data?
#2	Layer in transactional data and define target variable	CDW External customer demo- graphic data Transactional data	What are the transaction profiles of our customers? How do we define retention?	Overlay missing customer demographic data (2 hours) Land transactional data in analytic sandbox (4 hours) Profile and assess customer transaction data (40 hours) Create time series analysis for transactional data (60 hours)	How much transactional history do we need?
TBD					How should we define the holdout period?

period. A constraint that many teams encounter is that static data, such as customer attributes, is current state only. I may know that you live in Connecticut today, but may have no way of knowing that you lived in California prior to the holdout period. Data limitations like this are important to discuss with your stakeholders. Many times, the cost of trying to go back and create the data history isn't worthwhile. If it's identified as a serious limitation to the analysis, it may be a decision point for the organization to either stop the project or to remedy the situation.

SUMMARY

The analytic Scrum team meets with its business customers at the end of the sprint for a review session. During the session, the team shares analyses and data profiling examples, and receives clarification and feedback from the stakeholders. As an output of the review session, new stories or tasks may be added to the product backlog for prioritization. In the next sprint planning session, the product owner works with the team to prioritize the stories for the next sprint, and the team repeats the process of decomposing stories into tasks. As the team works through subsequent sprints, it captures and synthesizes additional data sources, performs statistical analysis, and creates a shared understanding with business stakeholders. Each review session provides a checkpoint on the continued viability of the project.

CHAPTER 15

Building in Quality and Simplicity

While agile methods are designed to build product quality within all of its processes, an overall quality management approach is important to your analytic project. Quality management encompasses strategies for planning, assurance, and control (see Figure 15.1). For the analytic team, this can take the form of design and development standards and testing strategies. Agile teams use a variety of quality approaches similar to teams using traditional software development methodologies. What is unique in agile is not necessarily the quality process itself, but how it is incorporated into the analytic lifecycle. This chapter provides an introduction to project quality management, practices, and testing approaches that any analytic project team can leverage.

QUALITY PLANNING

Quality management plays an important role in the analytic lifecycle. Quality management activities represent a broad set of functions to proactively plan for and monitor product quality. Quality management processes help the project team ensure that the project deliverable meets its intended purpose. The impact of a "bad" predictive

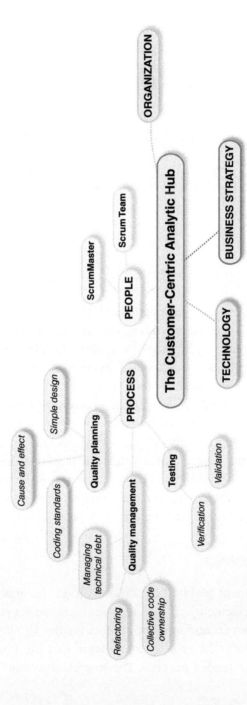

Figure 15.1 Quality Considerations

model can be disruptive to the organization in many ways: at worst, contributing to a loss of revenue or increased risk; at best, reducing the credibility of not only the team, but the ability of the business to trust future models. The analytic team should strive for perfection in technical and analytic execution.

Teams need to determine the cost of quality in terms of conformance or nonconformance. For example, money spent conforming proactively reduces the chance of a quality issue, while nonconformance costs are a result of fixing a quality issue. Conformance may include the cost of training, setting up the right infrastructure, testing, and inspections, while nonconformance costs include rework, lost business, lost time, and negative customer perception.

> Isabel sits down with Jeremy. "The quality of our analytics is really important to us. I firmly believe that if we agree on a consistent set of quality standards as we design and implement our analytic projects, we'll deliver a high-quality output to our customer as well as have a positive impact on the company's bottom line. If we can't execute or execute poorly, then that hurts our credibility and the credibility of the analysis that we provide.
>
> "I worked at a company once where the analytic team didn't have any standards in place. One of the team members created a model to evaluate the risk of loan default for customers. They modeled against an incorrect data source, used techniques that weren't peer reviewed by the team, but the model still went into production. Because the model couldn't accurately predict risk, the company lost millions of dollars. So you see, a few good practices up front can save us a lot of grief down the road.
>
> "But what we don't want to do is put in so many controls that we can't get work done. As a team, we came together and brainstormed all of the causes of poor model output and created a cause-and-effect diagram. Here, let me show you." Isabel pulls out a sheet of paper, shown in Figure 15.2. "We used the diagram as an input to developing our quality assurance processes and practices. In our case, we defined poor quality model deliverable as a model that had technical errors (data issues) or was not well received by the business."

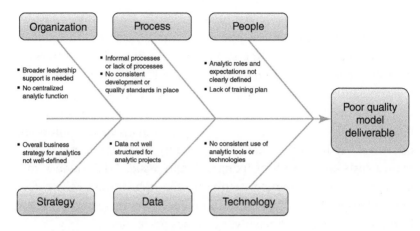

Figure 15.2 Analytic Cause-and-Effect Diagram

Quality assurance processes ensure that the team can satisfy organizational and project quality standards. In a traditional project, the team may create a quality assurance plan outlining purpose and scope, how reviews and audits will be conducted, and metrics used to evaluate quality. The quality assurance approach is designed to prevent or mitigate the impact of defects during the analytic development process.

Quality assurance forms the basis of a continuous improvement strategy. Audits assist the team in improving performance whether on the current or future project. Quality audit objectives may include the following:

- Assessing good and best practices used
- Identifying the impact of nonconformance to quality standards
- Sharing of external best practices
- Improving quality processes designed to raise team productivity
- Creating inputs for the organization's quality knowledge base to improve quality standards

"Remember when I told you that we use a number of technical practices on our team? When we developed our team practices, we took a look at the recommendations provided in the eXtreme Programming methodology. The concepts relevant to us were Simple Design, Pair

Programming, Refactoring, Collective Code Ownership, and Coding Standards. Let me give you an overview of each of the areas. When you start to work with the team on a project, you'll get a better sense of how you can put these practices into play."

SIMPLE DESIGN

There is a famous quote, often attributed to Mark Twain: "If I'd had more time, I would have written a shorter letter." Agile analytic teams develop with simplicity as the goal. Simple designs are more easily extensible and anticipate future change.

> "As mathematicians," says Isabel, "sometimes we fall in love with a beautiful solution. But sometimes a beautiful solution doesn't make a lot of sense to a business stakeholder. Even more importantly, we're not always efficient about the way we get to an answer. Sometimes our model development code looks like a lot of 'thinking out loud.' Our goal is to create analytic model workflows that are easy to adapt and simple to maintain as well as create models that maximize accuracy and explainability."

Shore and Warden (2008) advocate avoiding speculative coding; that is, analysts should ask themselves if further development supports the model design and features that need to be delivered. If the answer is no, then the code is better left alone. Code that is no longer in use should be removed as well. This is highly relevant in analytic project where statistical modelers are creating a lot of data ETL and model code in a number of different programming languages. This will help ensure that the design is right-sized and more easily understood. Additional simple design principles include:

> *Avoiding duplication* A core tenet of simple design is to avoid duplicitous code. XP promotes a "once and only once" approach to programming. Every concept within the code should have an explicit design representation. If the analytic team finds itself needing to reuse code (e.g., needing to consistently transform variables in a certain way or perform specific types of analysis on a repeated basis), that code should be externalized and called as needed.

Self-Documenting Code Simplicity is a subjective concept, so it's important that the programmers use a language or patterns familiar to the team in their design. Pair-programming is a technique used to overcome this problem: By ensuring that the code is understood by two different programmers, it's less likely to be misinterpreted by others. While it might seem counterintuitive, the need to comment code may indicate that the code is overly complex. The code should be expressive enough that comments are unnecessary. Another way to do this is to use software data mining tools that support self-documentation as the model is created.

Failing Fast A pitfall of simple design is that the design may be incomplete. Don't put hooks in to implement features or pull in data that aren't needed: You don't want to be stuck with unnecessary code that will become unfathomable to the analysts that come after you. In lieu of those unneeded hooks, write code to fail fast and prevent gaps from becoming a problem.

> "How we approach this," Isabel looks at Jeremy, "depends on the type of work that we're doing for our customers. If we're just doing some exploratory work to give the business some insight or direction, we probably won't worry as much about this level of rigor with the structure of the code, as long as the output is justifiable and accurate. However, if the model becomes productionalized—that is, it's going to be implemented in some other business application—we go back through a rigorous quality process to ensure that the code is streamlined and efficient. One thing that we realized is that most of our modelers are brilliant statisticians, but aren't always the best at writing production quality code. The good news is that we have some different people on our team with the skills that help us with that work."

Simple design relies on a continuous improvement mindset that leverages refactoring and incremental development. Modelers and analysts need to ensure that the design evolves with requirements. As noted in the quote about writing a shorter letter, it often takes more effort to do something that's simple, so simple shouldn't equate to fast or easy. Consider the simplest design that could possibly work.

CODING STANDARDS

Good teams agree on coding standards at the start of their project. These standards provide the guidelines that the analysts will agree to adhere to during development. Shore and Warden (2008) recommend that the team apply two guidelines: creating a minimal set of standards that the team can live with (don't get stuck arguing about formatting!), and focusing on consistency and consensus over perfection.

Some teams start with programming language specific industry-standard guides. Using these guides for basic formatting practices will help the team focus on design attributes. Starting discussion points for the team could include:

- Development and coding practices
- Documentation and annotation
- File and directory layouts
- Design and build conventions
- Error handling
- Modeling methodologies and techniques
- Pair programming
- Regulatory requirements

Pair programming (Shore and Warden, 2008) is a technique where two programmers work side by side. One programmer—the driver—codes, and the other—the navigator—watches, thinks, and provides feedback. This allows the driver to concentrate on developing code, and the navigator can be focused on the strategic issues. Pairing also promotes good programming habits and techniques by facilitating positive peer pressure during development. Pairs share best practices, knowledge, and experience as they perform their work—many pairs report fewer errors than when they work alone!

> "Okay," laughs Isabel, "when we instituted this practice, a lot of the modelers were really annoyed. Most of them like to work by themselves. So we made the practice optional for small projects, but mandatory on new projects and for new analysts on the team. Since you're new, I'm going to partner you up with one of our more experienced analysts as a mentor. This doesn't mean that your mentor will

breathe down your neck as you do your work—the two of
you will trade off. This will give you the opportunity to
share ideas and techniques, and will also help ensure
quality."

Pair programming is a useful technique that can be utilized when
the team is working on a high-priority or visibility project to help
ensure the quality of the results. Pairs aren't assigned, but come
together fluidly and rotate as needed. By keeping pairs shifting, the
team will increase its collective understanding of the work being
performed. Pairs swap driver/navigator roles frequently.

Shore and Warden (2008) recommends the following pairing tips:

- Pair on anything that needs to be maintained.
- Don't assign pairs—let them come together naturally.
- Switching partners will help with a fresh perspective.
- Avoid pairing with the same person every day.
- Produce code through collaborative conversation.
- Navigator and driver roles should be frequently rotated.

REFACTORING

Refactoring is the process of changing code design without changing
what the code does. Refactoring enables reflective design—the art of
improving on the design of existing code. Modelers and ETL specialists
can look for refactoring opportunities by sniffing out "code smells"—or
common design flaws in their model data preparation or model development code.

Good reflective design requires that the team understands the
existing design. If there's an expert on the team, have the expert
give a whiteboard session to the other data preparation specialists or
data scientists to walk through the process. If no one understands
the design (which may be the case if you're evaluating something
that was developed long ago), start your own analysis by working
back through the original design: look at responsibilities, interactions,
and dependencies. While reflective design gives guidance on what

to change, it's refactoring that enables that change. Refactoring is performed in a series of small, incremental steps—a large change to the data preparation or model development code may encompass several individual refactorings. Refactoring is an ongoing process throughout the analytic development lifecycle that helps the team continually validate and improve the ongoing usability of the design.

COLLECTIVE CODE OWNERSHIP

By collectively owning code and models, the team shares the responsibility and ownership for the quality of the code and models. No single analyst or modeler owns code, and code changes can be made by anyone on the team. This practice helps mitigate the risk of having one person with all of the knowledge, and has the benefit of improving code quality.

The practices of collective code ownership and refactoring are designed to leave the code a little better than you found it. The concept of collective ownership requires the team to jointly commit to producing good code. Analysts are expected to write the best code they possibly can, but it doesn't mean they have to be perfect. Do your best work, and if it needs improvement, other team members (modelers, analysts, developers) can make adjustments when the time is right.

Communication is essential to collective code ownership. This helps the team members maintain their shared vision. The combination of other technical practices like simple design, coding standards, and refactoring will help make collective ownership easier. Changes to code and models are coordinated through the practice of continuous integration and version control.

> "I know it sounds like a lot to remember, but all of these practices help us reduce our technical debt."
>
> Jeremy looks puzzled. "What's that?"
>
> "Technical debt," says Isabel, "is all the shortcuts that you take to get work done, but aren't sustainable. It's all the quick and dirty fixes that you put in to get something to work, but make it unmanageable in the future."

TECHNICAL DEBT

Technical debt contributes to increased maintenance costs down the road as it makes models more difficult to maintain (think of all of the unmanageable legacy code out there!). Model code with a large technical debt may be cheaper to rebuild than modify down the road.

> "I remember when I started here. There were a whole bunch of propensity models that had been created and were being used to support the marketing organization. A number of those models were running in production and were generating scores that were being used to implement marketing campaigns. The business saw a decline in its response rate and wanted us to check the models. It was my responsibility to go through and figure out what the models were doing. There was no documentation and the code was a mess! I ended up completely rebuilding and revalidating those models from scratch. Never again!" Isabel pounds the desk with her fist, laughing.

The technical debt quadrant in Figure 15.3 (Fowler, 2009) outlines the deliberate and accidental ways that teams can take on debt.

Prudent debt is generally taken on deliberately. The team knows that technical debt exists, but chooses not to deal with it. In this case,

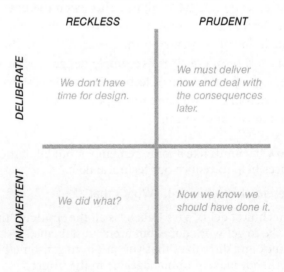

Figure 15.3 Technical Debt Quadrant

the economic (or time) trade-off between the payoff and the paydown of the debt doesn't make sense. Prudent-inadvertent technical debt can occur when the team retrospectively analyzes its work—for example, let's say the team delivers working code or design, but after it's been developed, the team realized that there might be a better way to do it.

Reckless-deliberate debt manifests itself in "cowboy coding"—or quick and dirty work that's performed just to get the job done. The team knows that it could be better, but makes a conscious decision to write poorly designed or messy code. Reckless-inadvertent debt may happen when the team isn't skilled in good coding or design practices.

TESTING

Testing helps the team deliver output that meets organizational and customer standards. Data scientists play a critical role in the quality process by debugging their code: making sure that individual sections of code in the model development process perform as expected. This is especially important to modelers who might be creating their models in a variety of programming languages or across different data or technology platforms. Unit tests are small, simple tests written to see if a returned value is the value expected. The test isolates the function from the rest of the code to determine whether the function performs as expected (basically, did the code you write meet the expected results).

In addition to testing components of a model development workflow, code should be integration tested. Integration testing tests the interoperability of multiple systems or subsystems and is an extension of unit testing. Using a bottom-up approach, unit tests are combined into modules or builds and subsequently tested together. Top-down integration tests test modules and then decompose testing to the unit level. Both unit and integration tests test functionality.

In model development, integration testing is particularly important in the ETL used to prepare the modeling dataset since most teams are aggregating data from disparate sources. Unit and integration testing help ensure that data are appropriately aggregated and transformed through the modeling process. This activity will be less important for teams using a stable analytic dataset for their modeling work, since the quality assurance processes should have been completed in the creation of that file. However, if a team is adding external data sources to a base modeling table, then the data flow should be integration tested.

As errors (or "bugs") are uncovered through the testing process, bugs are captured within a defect tracking system (for a simple system, this could be an Excel spreadsheet, or a defect or quality management software application may be used for complex systems). The analytic team must actively assess, prioritize, and manage bugs, which will primarily take the shape of data quality defects.

Verification and Validation

Verification and validation are two key components of testing. Verification ensures that the deliverable meets design specifications, while validation ensures that the deliverable meets user expectations. Validation of the model development process comes in the form of validating the business understanding of the data.

> Isabel says to Jeremy: "We were working on this project last month and we built this great product acquisition model for the marketing team. We'd done all of our verification work and the model was technically accurate. When we sat down with our customer, we found out that we had misinterpreted the business meaning of some key variables. The problem was that these variables popped out as being the most predictive. We had to go back to the drawing board. We're trying to get better about identifying those issues upfront, but it's not always possible, especially when we're working on a new project. But as we find things, we do document them and put them in our knowledge repository. I'll show you that later.

> "As you can see," Isabel continues, "quality and testing are really important to us. We don't wait until the end of the project to check our work. If we waited until the end and we find errors, there's a big risk that rework will significantly impact any deadlines we have or the cost of our resources. Our system of checks and balances means that the earlier we find something, the less impact it is to fix. For each new project, we meet with our customer and discuss our testing approach."

SUMMARY

Quality management strategies remain an important part of any project regardless of the delivery methodology. Quality management encompasses a broad spectrum of planning, assurance, and control activities. Proactive planning processes are often aligned to internal and external quality standards. Quality assurance forms the basis of the team's project quality methods while quality control helps ensure that the project output meets customer requirements. The team leverages technical development practices in performing the work, which may include coding standards, test-driven development approaches, refactoring, pair programming, and other methods. These technical best practices help the team minimize technical debt. Testing forms an integral part of the quality plan by reducing risk and uncovering defects.

CHAPTER **16**

Collaboration and Communication

gile teams set up their environment for success. The team's physical and virtual space provides a critical area for the team to effectively communicate, collaborate, and share information between the team and customers. But there's no one right way to configure a space, and working with your team members to find out what works best for them in your operational environment is important (see Figure 16.1).

THE TEAM SPACE

As a follow-on to The Agile Manifesto, the authors defined 12 supporting principles behind the Manifesto. One of the principles states: "The most efficient and effective method of conveying information to and within a development team is face-to-face conversation" (Beck, Beedle, Bennekum, et al., 2001). Agile promotes high-bandwidth communications—that is, the environment supports the exchange of information quickly and efficiently across the project team. This results in an increase in both the frequency and quality of information shared.

The team's environment needs to support collaboration. A common setup for a project team might be in a dedicated "war" room:

191

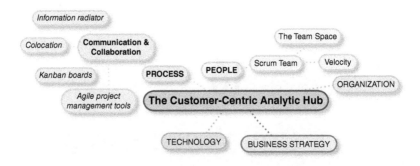

Figure 16.1 Collaboration and Communication Considerations

Agile teams often have a dedicated open room that the team works in. Desks or tables are configured to be collaboration-friendly with minimal barriers (such as walls or dividers) to facilitate interaction and conversation.

> Isabel looks at the office plans the designer has brought her. "This looks good," she thinks, "this new configuration is really going to help the team communicate better." The plan includes a series of lower walled cubicles that allow for privacy, but are configured around an open space. A separate dedicated team "war room" is off to the side. Before working with the design on the plans, Isabel met with her team to discuss their options.
>
> Isabel came to the team with the open space concept and was met with stony silence. "All right team, what's the problem?"
>
> One of the analysts spoke up. "The data and the statistical work we do is really intense. I work best when I have access to a quiet space to complete my work. I think the open space will be noisy and disruptive—or worse, it will make us all feel self-conscious about the noise, and we'll be afraid to talk!"
>
> "Good points," Isabel says. "Let's brainstorm some ideas for making this a space where we can respect the need for quiet concentration, but also help us collaborate better."
>
> Sarah, one of the ETL developers, looked at the design. "I see spaces for our team, but what about dedicating some

space for our partners? Sometimes we work with business and IT people on pretty intense projects—it would be great to have an area where they could come and sit with us during the project. Also, in our old workspace, our data scientists were too far away from our team's ETL developers. If we could move those two groups closer together, I think that would be more efficient."

"I know it sounds hokey," Rebecca says, "but we shouldn't forget about team spirit. I like the idea of keeping a casual team space where we can hang out, relax, and have conversations. We also need a lot of visual communication tools—whiteboards and extra wall space—so that important team information can be displayed where everyone can see it."

The team's space is a living, breathing entity (see Figure 16.2). Agile projects are visible to the team and the stakeholders. The term "information radiator" (Cockburn, 2008) is used to describe the visual display of information in a team space. The information radiator is

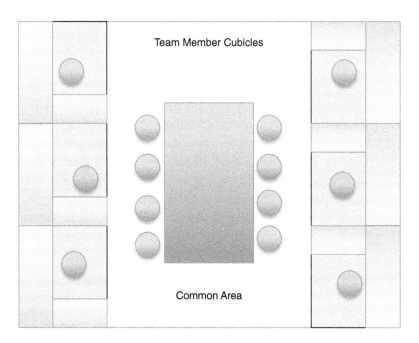

Figure 16.2 The Team Space

simply a visible space (wall, whiteboard) for the team to highlight their progress throughout their projects: The purpose is to provide up-to-date information about the project to the extended team.

> Isabel sketches a layout of the team space, and includes cubicles, an open area, and a conference room that will be turned into the team's war room. "All good?" she asked the team. "Yes!" they said. She turned the plans over to the designer.

Ideally, agile teams are co-located—all team members are in the same place. The modern reality is that this isn't possible for most organizations. Teams are split across buildings, geographic regions, countries, and time zones.

> The demand for Isabel's team's work is growing dramatically to the point where she needs to increase her staff. Isabel meets with her boss, who tells her: "We don't have the budget right now to increase our full-time staff. Our outsourcing partner has analytic resources available if we've got overflow work we can't handle."
>
> "Hmmm … " she thinks, "how are we going to coordinate our work across the teams?"

If your team is dispersed, it doesn't mean that you can't collaborate effectively—you just have to work harder at it. Most organizations have any number of collaboration platforms available at their disposal: video conferencing, knowledge management tools, agile project management tools, and social/collaboration tools, for example. Keep in mind that the capabilities are only as good as their usefulness to the team. We've found that these tools work best when the team members can determine which ones will best suit their collective needs. Remember to empower your team members and let them self-organize.

THINGS TO PUT IN THE INFORMATION RADIATOR

As the team's project coordinator, Rebecca works with the group to update the information on the team radiator. There are several big projects in progress, all slightly different, and she's trying to simplify the information so that each team can easily track progress and stay focused on its goals. Rebecca asks that each team provide the following information for the information radiator.

Project Vision Statement   This one-page document helps keep the team focused on the project and its importance to the organization.

User Personas   Several of the teams are working on customer segmentation projects. As teams uncover segments, they create user personas that describe the attributes of that segment.

Work Backlog   The work backlog is updated daily on a task or Kanban board. The backlog list includes additional analysis or exploration work required, a data backlog of information to be reviewed, and any data integration work.

Work Burndown Chart   During each iteration of work, the team updates the remaining work effort for each outstanding task. Buy tallying up the daily work estimates, the team has an easy way to visualize and communicate remaining work.

Data Defects   As the teams work through different data sources, they log any data-quality errors that might impact the work quality.

ANALYTIC VELOCITY

Teams measure the amount of work completed in a sprint by calculating their velocity. Velocity is calculated by adding up the size of the product backlog items completed at the sprint's finish. Partially completed product backlog items do not count in a team's velocity metric. Velocity measures the team's output, not the value of the output.

A team's velocity plays a critical role in Scrum planning processes. At the release level, the team adds up the total story points within a release and then divides that by the team's average velocity to come up with the number of sprints within the release. Velocity is also used as an input for evaluating and improving the team's processes. By reviewing velocity over time, the team can analyze the impact of process changes on its ability to deliver customer value.

A team's velocity can be charted in a work burndown chart. Figure 16.3 is a sample burndown chart that shows the progress of

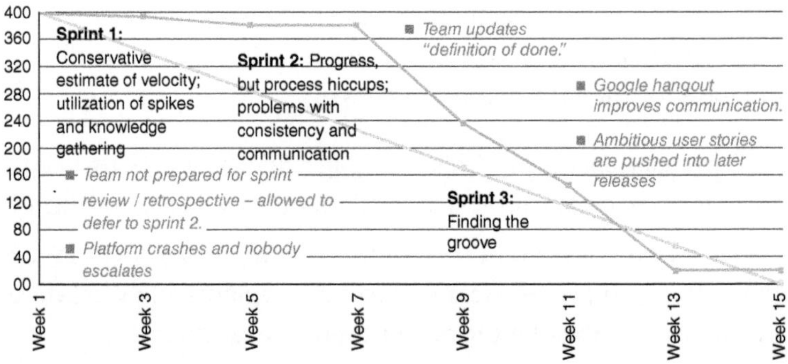

Figure 16.3 Analytic Sprint Burndown Chart

three two-week analytic sprints within a single release. Since this was the team's first time at using Scrum, the first two sprints were a little rocky. The burndown chart features the total number of estimated project hours on the *y*-axis of the chart and a timeline on the *x*-axis. The straight line is a linear representation of work, and the team's completed work effort (in story hours) is plotted against it. If the team's line is above the linear line, then the team is behind schedule. In our example, this team fell behind during the first two sprints, but caught up in sprint three.

IMPROVING VELOCITY

If teams are consistently inspecting and adapting their processes, they will likely see an improvement in their velocity. However, velocity typically plateaus at a certain point. Teams can still gain momentum by increasing training, using improved tools or even changing team composition. Managers should expect a slight temporary drop in velocity as the team gets up to speed while these changes are implemented.

Velocity is not comparable across teams, in part because each team may have a different sizing metric for product backlog items. Additionally, making teams compete on velocity results in behavior that's inconsistent with delivering customer value—teams may end up cutting corners to hit a target velocity number.

THE KANBAN OR TASK BOARD

Most agile teams organize their work on a task board. The task board includes each work backlog item that will be worked on during the sprint. The task board provides a real-time view into what work is remaining, what is in progress, and what has been completed. It can be as simple as a series of Post-It notes on a whiteboard or put into any number of Kanban-specific software applications.

Task boards help the team maintain flow and limit the amount of work-in-progress. Task boards are also referred to as Kanban boards, as shown in Figure 16.4. Kanban is a Japanese term used in lean "pull" systems. A pull system uses visual clues to inform the team that work is available and ready. All of the tasks start out in the to-do column, and then the team selects work to be performed, moving the task to the "in-progress" column. When the task is complete, it is moved to the "done" column. The board helps the team easily see what work has been completed, what needs to be done, and where the bottlenecks are.

Isabel's team manages multiple Kanban boards. There is one for each project, and then a separate one to reflect all the small day-to-day requests that come in.

"This is killing me!" Rebecca says to Isabel. "Maintaining all of these manual task boards and Post-It notes is a ton of work. Some of the teams aren't updating their boards frequently enough, either. Plus, when we start

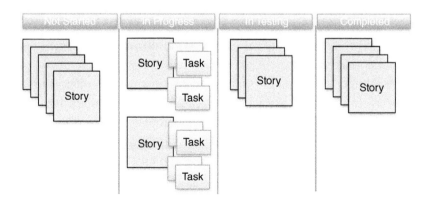

Figure 16.4 Analytic Kanban Board

to onboard the offshore resources, how are we going to communicate our work-in-progress and share information?"

"That's a good point." Isabel pauses for a minute. "The Kanban boards are really important to me—it gives me a great visual of what the teams are working on and what's left to do. I know it takes some effort to keep updated, but I've gotten feedback from the teams that they like having a clear picture of what they're doing. What other options do we have?"

"I've been doing some research." Rebecca pulls out her laptop. "There are agile project management applications that we can subscribe to. All of the data in our information radiator can be put into the application. I checked with our IT department; they're already using ABC Agile Software, and they said that we could have some of their licenses. Here, take a look."

"Good idea," says Isabel, poking around the screen. "Looks like there's some good features here. Let's get the IT group to give us a demo. Then we'll see if it's a good fit for us."

CONSIDERING AN AGILE PROJECT MANAGEMENT TOOL

When you're assessing a project management tool for your analytic team, focus on the aspects that are important to you. Most agile development applications are incredibly robust and may offer a lot of features that are nice but that the team won't really use. Keep in mind the concept of "minimally sufficient": What do you need to get your job done more easily?

Most agile development tools include the ability to plan at multiple levels: portfolio, project, release, and iteration. Enterprise class applications will have deep test management capabilities. Some platforms include the ability to create and manage more visual tools, such as roadmaps or storyboards. Reporting and metrics are also important capabilities. These tools can be helpful in managing your agile analytic project, but come with administrative overhead that the team needs to account for when assessing the benefit of the tool.

Activities like setting up permissions, user management, and system configuration can cause a lot of overhead for the team. Since each analytic and development team will have a different workflow, some amount of effort will go into customizing the tool to fit your business process.

Centralized agile tools offer many benefits to the team. Team members can see their assigned tasks, track time, and look at trends such as their velocity and burndown charts. These tools also ensure that valuable data are well categorized and do not get lost. An audit trail and version control is also helpful for understanding when changes are being made and by whom. Users can access the application concurrently, which helps avoid bottlenecks in updating information.

Overall, large tools like this are most beneficial to teams that can accommodate the overhead of managing them. Ideally, that burden is shared between multiple agile teams that do work the same way. The security of having your data on a centralized secure server is one of the most important benefits.

> Isabel sets up a demo with the IT team. A ScrumMaster from one of the development teams shows them an in-flight project that they're working on.
>
> "One of the aspects of the tool we really like," he says, "is that we work on a distributed, geographically dispersed team. We absolutely needed some type of tool to facilitate communication. What I will tell you is that we definitely get more detail and a better understanding of what's going on in our one-to-one conversations. We've struggled a little bit with figuring out how to capture our 'hallway conversations' in the tool. Those informal meetings generate a lot of insight and context. We try to do the best we can at updating our tool with that information, but we need to get better at it. What you get out of the tool is only as good as what you put into it. As a result, we end up with a delayed state of information sometimes. The balance is that you also don't want to be a slave to the tool—if we're spending more time updating the tool than doing actual work, that's a problem.
>
> "Now, if you were the only team that was going to use this application, I would recommend going with

something simpler. But since it's supported by IT—we have a big user community and lots of onboarding and training sessions—we can help you focus on just using the parts of the application that are going to give you the most value. I also think this will be a really big help when the analytics team starts to do more integrated work with our application development team. We'll all be working off of the same set of information. Now let's find a project that we can put in here for you as a pilot. That will help you decide whether you want to use the tool for all of your projects moving forward."

"Great idea!" says Isabel. "I know just the project to start with. But does it matter if our agile workflow is different from yours?"

"Not at all," he replies, "we'll set up the functionality that works for you. When we get to the point where we're linking projects across IT and analytics, you can still keep your process. We'll just manage it at the release level."

"What's a release?" she asks.

He laughs, "Oh, I forgot, that's an IT term. Your group has been working in sprints, right?" Isabel nods. "Well, a release is what happens when you get through a certain number of sprints and you're ready to release functionality to your customer. You might not have a formal release with your analytic projects today. We coordinate releases across all the different groups that might be working on a project. How you do the work is up to you—when it gets coordinated and released is up to us."

SUMMARY

Agile teams create an environment that facilitates the flow of information across the team and to customers. The teams often work in a designated "war room," a dedicated space that the team shares and allows them to focus on the work at hand with minimal external disruptions. The team communicates progress on an information radiator within the physical or virtual team space: The information radiator includes charts and visuals such as the task board, progress charts, and other essential project material. The team establishes a sustainable pace of work captured in a metric called velocity, an important input into the planning process. Agile project management tools can facilitate the collection and dissemination of project information, but watch out for creating unnecessary processes that interfere with the team's ability to complete their most important work.

CHAPTER 17

Business
Implementation
Planning

A s the team hits the third release, it prepares to deliver the final model results to the business. By keeping to the release schedule, the team avoids overdelivering and overanalyzing. The analytic team develops a formal presentation to present the finalized results: Remember that the team has been sharing preliminary results and findings throughout the project, so nothing presented should be a surprise to the stakeholders. For some analytic teams, their work might end at this phase of the project, but staying engaged during business implementation planning has benefits for both the analytic group and the stakeholders (see Figure 17.1).

ARE WE DONE YET?

Everyone asks: How do we know when our model development phase is really complete? There are two aspects of this—the first is that you must always be cognizant of your business's ability to consume the model output. Don't spend your time creating 10 predictive models when your business can only handle the implementation complexity of 1 model.

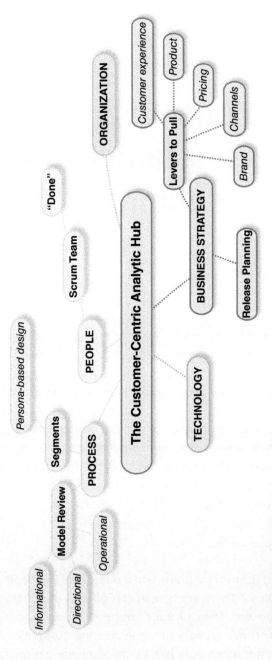

Figure 17.1 Business Implementation Planning Considerations

As an example, one organization with a renewal membership product wanted to create a predictive model to identify customers at risk of non-renewing their membership. They already knew that the churn rate after the first year was very high and then continually dropped in each subsequent renewal year (i.e., the longer you're a member, the more likely you are to renew). Before beginning to create the churn model, the data scientist clustered the membership base and identified three distinct populations—customers in the first year of their membership; customers who were members for two to five years; and customers who were members longer than five years. Since this was this organization's very first time using predictive models, only two models were recommended: customers in the first year of their membership and customers in the two to five year membership period. As the organization becomes more comfortable using the model output, it can increase the granularity and number of models produced down the road.

Model development is not a once-and-done activity. In this example, the organization wanted to create predictive models for a number of different customer scenarios. But for the first iteration of the project, it didn't make sense: It didn't have any operational mechanism to handle the complexity of running multiple models in production, or managing and tracking multiple propensity scores. It also lacked the ability to create and manage treatment strategies for all of those models. You shouldn't be trying to create perfection in your first iteration; build on your capabilities and capture ideas for future projects on your idea backlog.

What's Next?

Most analytic teams narrowly focus on the development and production of the model, often forgetting that their business partners need guidance in how that model, score, segment, and so on can be used to influence behavior. This is why many analytic projects fail to meet their original business objectives. Even worse, business stakeholders may not understand how to interpret or use the analysis. Just because you can predict an event doesn't mean that you can influence the outcome.

So our analytic team's work isn't over yet: In fact, it's just beginning! The analysts' knowledge and skill are essential in the development of the business implementation strategy, but an important note here: While the business users continuously engage with the analytic team throughout the project and have started to think of some areas where the models and segments could be used, the final results of the modeling activity are needed to solidify the strategy. This is because treatment strategies are specific to the final output. Until you know what that is, it's difficult to define in advance. Ideas that are generated during the modeling process can be put on an idea backlog; or if there is enough information uncovered in the data and model development phases to move forward with creating mockup implementation plans for a particular business treatment, go for it!

ANALYTIC RELEASE PLANNING

At the end of release three, *Model Hardening*, Isabel's team is ready to release the finalized analytic results to the business stakeholders. In advance of the release, Rebecca sets up a half-day session to review the final models and segments with the team. In advance of the meeting, the analytic team prepares a document that provides a business representation of the model output—a simplified, easily understood document that highlights the data sources used, the model development process, and the model results. The document is important because you want the results to be easily understood: This means that if someone picks up the document without an explanation, he or she would understand the work that's been performed as well as any limitations or organizational decision points that happened along the way.

The team prepares the presentation for the release meeting, as shown in Figure 17.2.

Section 1: What Did We Do, and Why?

In this section, provide a brief one-page overview of the project. Document any assumptions or business decisions that influenced the development of the models. (Example: Why did we create two models instead of three?). If some particular analysis requested by a business

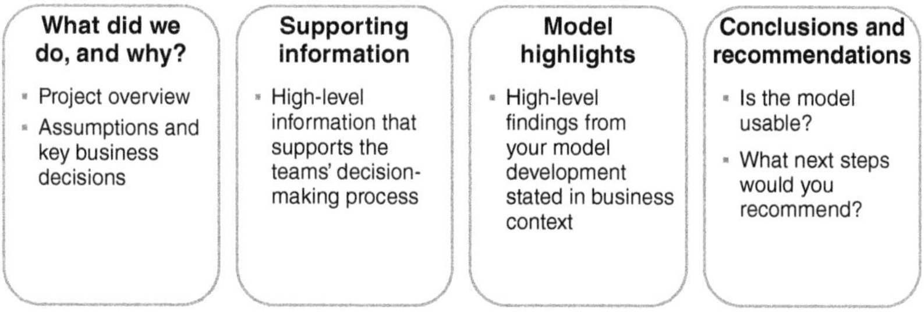

What did we do, and why?	Supporting information	Model highlights	Conclusions and recommendations
▪ Project overview ▪ Assumptions and key business decisions	▪ High-level information that supports the teams' decision-making process	▪ High-level findings from your model development stated in business context	▪ Is the model usable? ▪ What next steps would you recommend?

Figure 17.2 Analytic Release Presentation

stakeholder was deferred to a later iteration or release, state why. Remember that you are likely to have business stakeholders who are looking to discredit your analytic work for any number of reasons. Including this information helps the broader business community understand what decisions were made and why. Also include a definitions section—sometimes the work that you do changes assumptions that a businessperson might have (e.g., analytic work might identify a new definition for an "occasional" customer based on statistical techniques—this definition might be fundamentally different from the business definition).

By laying out your work in the following way, you're acknowledging and addressing business stakeholder concerns about why you made certain decisions during the development process. This information should not be any different from input captured during sprint reviews; but it's helpful as a reminder. Often, through your stakeholder management process, you've identified all the people relevant to your immediate project. Once the work has been completed, your primary stakeholders begin to share information with secondary stakeholder groups—people who have not been involved in the day-to-day aspects of the project, but may be influential players in your rollout strategy. For example, if the model pointed to information that pointed to changing payment options as a way to influence retention rates, and the team responsible for billing wasn't part of the project, then there might be some resistance. This is okay—you can't always identify every stakeholder upfront in a project, but at least have a concise document on hand so that you can easily explain the project and your process for arriving at a given conclusion.

Section 2: Supporting Information

In this section, include any relevant graphs or information that support the team's decision-making process for model development. Only include information that helps tell your story—extra detail should be put in the appendix.

Section 3: Model Highlights

Provide high-level bullet points on the findings from each model that the team has developed. Focus on what's explainable from a business perspective. You'll need to distill it down to information your stakeholders can understand. For example, let's say you've built a series of models using different statistical techniques. The recommended scoring models are based on logistic regression techniques; however, the decision tree models are close in their predictability of the target and are used as a means to interpret the relationship of the variables to the target. Again, make sure the information you present fits the audience.

Section 4: Conclusions and Recommendations

Add any conclusions you have about the model here. Is the model performing well enough to use operationally? What else can you conclude from the results? Remember that the model propensity scores are only one mechanism that can be used; separate treatments can be designed around the individual model variables as well.

Keep your presentation short and to the point. Provide enough information for discussion and interpretation during your release session. The point of this session is to identify ways to use the models and segments. As you present your content, start capturing questions, thoughts, and ideas from your business stakeholder community.

Throughout the modeling process, you'll likely uncover patterns in customer behavior that start to form a *customer journey*—that is, one or many paths that a customer may take to arrive at a particular outcome. As you identify these paths, look for areas where your analytics can be used to influence that outcome.

Section 5: Appendix

Use this area to include any detailed information on the project.

In our retention example, through the development process the team uncovered a high percentage of missing demographic variables, including customer age. The team was able to overlay the missing data with third-party information. The age variable turned out to be the most predictive variable in the model. One of the team's first recommendations might be to improve the collection of that variable so that it didn't have to rely on less accurate information.

Another interesting finding is that several of the variables in the model are available at the time a customer first makes a purchase. So instead of trying to reach out to customers after we've already lost them, we can make a good determination at the time they first purchase on their likelihood to churn. This gives us a longer runway to turn them into long-term customers.

MODEL REVIEW

The team gets together during the release session to review the final model and segmentation output and outlay a rough implementation strategy. The first hour of the meeting is used to walk through the final model results. The analytic team walks the business stakeholders through the final business representation of the model output. The team showcases the segments that emerged during the modeling exercise. With the analytic work complete, the group begins to discuss if and how the analytics (insights, models, and segments) can be integrated into the business.

In many organizations, the analytic team's work stops once the analytic output is delivered to the end customer (in this case, the project sponsor and business stakeholders). However, it can be extremely beneficial for the analytic team to stay engaged with the stakeholders through this part of the project lifecycle to ensure that the output is used appropriately in support of these broader business objectives. By actively participating in this process, the analytic team also gains a deeper understanding of the business context, which is useful for future projects.

Levers to Pull

As the organization determines how to use the model propensity scores and segments, there are many business levers that can be pulled. Model-specific strategies should be tied to variables in the model. For example, if the most predictive variables in our churn model are tied to transaction frequency, proximity to a retail store, or amount spent, treatment strategies should be designed to influence those variables. In this case, the organization might consider the placement of their retail stores, their product lineup, or perhaps pricing. Some of the treatment strategies might require additional models or analysis (e.g., What is the optimal mix of products in my stores that would raise my average transaction amount?)—and that's fine. Those models and ideas can go back onto an idea backlog for future prioritization.

Figure 17.3 outlines five basic areas that ABP is considering as it is developing the implementation strategy for the analytic project. The categories for your analytic project may look different, based on your particular business needs.

> *Product Development* Analytics provide great input into product development strategies. In our retention example, maybe our customers aren't buying our products anymore because we don't offer the right products. Or perhaps we have the right product and the wrong target audience.

> *Pricing* Pricing is the most critical component of any business strategy. How do we determine a price that will maximize both

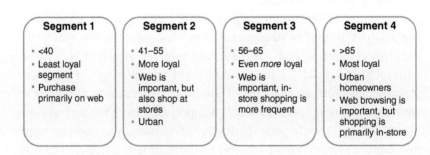

Figure 17.3 ADP Customer Segments

customer loyalty and company profitability? Beyond the price of an item, service, and so on, are there different payment plans that we could offer? One organization found that its retention rate rose dramatically when it offered installment payment options on its service.

Distribution Channels There are more distribution channel options than ever before. Are you offering your product or service through the channels that customers want to interact with you in? For example, if you only interact with your customer over the phone but your competitors allow customers to complete transactions over web or mobile, you are at a disadvantage.

Marketing and Brand Analytics are enormously helpful in driving marketing and brand strategies. Response models can help identify which customers are more likely to respond to a particular offer or message and create brand awareness.

Customer Experience and Loyalty Models can help business understand the drivers behind customer experience and loyalty by determining how customers behaviorally respond to your business.

As you go through your analytic project, you may have a particular area of focus, such as redefining a pricing strategy or improving marketing campaigns. However, be open to other areas where your analytics could be used to influence other business strategies.

PERSONA-BASED DESIGN

As ABP's analytic team progressed through their project, the analytic work uncovered some interesting segments in its customer base.

> With the model development complete, the project team gets together to discuss how to leverage the insights generated throughout the development process and the churn propensity scores.
>
> Isabel walks the group through some of the findings. "As the team created the predictive models, we identified several distinct customer clusters. This is some of the work that you've already seen in our sprint reviews. One of the primary differentiators in retention is that younger people

tend to be less loyal and they're more likely to shop on our website versus our retail stores. But you can see that as the customers age, they become more loyal and begin to migrate toward retail. In fact, as you can see, we ended up with four age-group clusters. In each group, the next most predictive attribute is how they interact with us, followed by other demographic and behavioral predictors. So in addition to the likelihood to churn scores, we can start to think about some different treatment strategies for these different groups."

Whether your model development process identifies natural segments in the population, or your analytic project is specific to customer segmentation, you can use these predictive attributes to define strategies and tactics specific to those customer communities. A great technique to use as the next starting point is *persona-based design*.

Persona-based design helps you take an outward-in perspective to understanding and responding to customer needs. The persona, a hypothetical customer, represents a particular customer segment within your business. By understanding your customers' needs from their perspective, you can begin to outline approaches for more effectively managing the relationship with that customer group.

ABP's predictive attrition model uncovered four customer segments. As each segment increases in age, its likelihood to churn decreases. Figure 17.3 outlines some simple customer profile information for each segment.

Each one of these segments can be used to create a customer persona. While segments might give you insight into **who** a person is, personas can start to capture **why** they're behaving a certain way (see Figure 17.4). Segmentation and persona development techniques incorporate aspects of both predictive and descriptive analysis. As you gain more sophistication in your segmentation strategies, you'll often have customers in multiple segments (demographic, behavioral, engagement profile).

This progressive elaboration from segment to persona helps the team develop ways to engage with "Jennifer" differently and encourage loyalty.

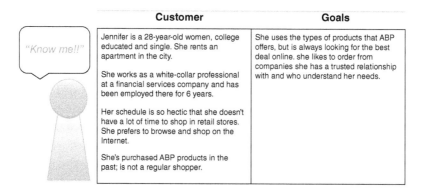

	Customer	Goals
"Know me!!"	Jennifer is a 28-year-old women, college educated and single. She rents an apartment in the city. She works as a white-collar professional at a financial services company and has been employed there for 6 years. Her schedule is so hectic that she doesn't have a lot of time to shop in retail stores. She prefers to browse and shop on the Internet. She's purchased ABP products in the past; is not a regular shopper.	She uses the types of products that ABP offers, but is always looking for the best deal online. she likes to order from companies she has a trusted relationship with and who understand her needs.

Figure 17.4 ABP Customer Persona for Segment One

Segmentation Case Study

Let's look at a simple banking case study (see Figure 17.5). The bank has more than 100 customer propensity models in their warehouse. It overlays lifestage segments with other propensity model scores that are aligned with particular bank objectives to identify market opportunities.

This segmentation strategy is designed to put customers in consistent groups based on needs and wants so that the bank can develop segment-specific solutions. Using these segments, the bank identified several different customer lifestages and specific needs that customers have within those lifestages.

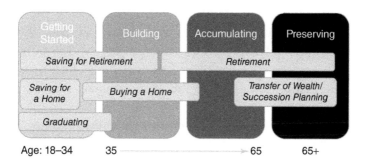

Figure 17.5 Banking Case Study Customer Lifestages and Needs

The analytic team at the bank creates both strategic and tactical models. The strategic models focus on customer priorities, including profitability, lifestage, profit potential, retention/loyalty, and risk. The tactical models focus on lead generation and revenue: propensity to buy, propensity to use financial products, and so on.

In one analytic exercise, the bank found opportunity in a sub-segment. It noticed a travel pattern for certain customer traveling from the north to the south of the United States during the winter. It created a special "snowbird" package that bundled travel insurance and other financial products, and provided a dedicated customer service line. Additionally, it created a referral program for getting those customers into local bank outlets in their vacation locations. The outcome was higher per average products per client, a 45 percent decrease in attrition, and increased profitability within the sub-segment.

The message here is that you may have some logical customer segments based on typical business rules, or you might find interesting new segments or sub-segments within your predictive analysis to target. While it might not happen in every modeling exercise, ADP found distinct customer clusters in its attrition modeling. As it is defining the implementation strategy, each cluster has a different set of treatments.

SUMMARY

The analytic team wraps up its model delivery release by packaging its findings and results to present to the business stakeholders. While the analytic team might consider its work complete by the end of the release, it is recommended that the team stay engaged throughout the business implementation planning process. The purpose is twofold: The analytic group shares how the results are best used to define treatment strategies, and the team gains an appreciation of the business context in which the analysis is used. Once the model review is complete, the organization considers what business levers can be pulled to influence better outcomes. Persona-based design is a good technique for teasing out which treatment strategies will be most effective.

CHAPTER **18**

Building Agility into Test-and-Learn Strategies

O nce your predictive models are created and your treatment strategies defined, it's time to create your test-and-learn strategy. Just because you can predict that an event is likely to occur, your ability to influence that event is unknown. Test-and-learn approaches are important in helping to understand which treatments and tactics will be most effective in influencing outcomes across your segments. Think of test-and-learn as a disciplined way to experiment and innovate: The faster you can speed up your experimentation cycles, the more quickly you'll be able to adapt and respond. While we won't be able to do justice to this important topic in one chapter, we'll provide an overview of things to consider in your predictive modeling project (see Figure 18.1).

WHAT IS TEST-AND-LEARN?

Test-and-learn strategies have been prevalent in marketing organizations for decades and have been expanded more broadly into other

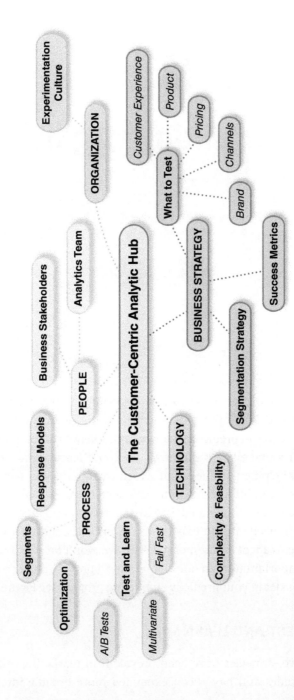

Figure 18.1 Agility Test and Learn Considerations

areas of the business, such as pricing or product development. Just like with our product backlog, a typical test-and-learn cycle starts with a hypothesis. But in this case, our hypotheses center around different ideas we have for influencing our customers' behavior: For example, you might believe that customers will respond to a certain offer or message over another.

This is the same approach that Isabel's team employed at the start of its project when it created its hypothesis backlog. A hypothesis test provides a way to statistically validate assumptions around a particular business question or idea. Hypothesis testing gives us a simple way to test the validity of our intuition using data. In a simple example, you may use what's called an A/B or split test: a randomized experiment with two (or more) variants, a control and a treatment group(s).

> Natasha reviews a decile chart of the model scores with the operations and marketing groups. "You can see from this chart that about 20 percent of our customer base is at high risk of never buying any of our products again. One of the influential variables in our model indicated that people who respond to our email offers are less like to leave. Marketing is going to execute a series of special email campaigns to target that group of customers." She continues, "We're going to take all of the customers who have an at-risk propensity score of 75 percent or greater and use a 10 percent control sample. The control group won't get a special offer. Our treatment group will get one of two offers. The control group is randomly sampled, and the treatment group will be randomly sampled to receive a particular message."

	Treatment Group: At-Risk Customers	Control Group (10% sample)
Population	9,000	1,000
Responses	355	N/A
Message A: In-store coupon (50%)	153 (3.4% response rate)	N/A
Message B: Online discount (50%)	202 (4.5% response rate)	N/A

Let's say you have a new email campaign targeted to our "at-risk" customers announcing a special sale, and you want to test different messages. Your at-risk population is randomly split into two groups, treatment and control. The treatment group received an offer, and the control group receives nothing.

The team assigns each offer in the treatment group with a special code, so when the customer uses the coupon or discount, it's tracked in an operational system and can be analyzed. The team decides to put a two-week time dimension on the offer so that it can begin to track results quickly. After the campaign is executed, the team evaluates the responses to see which group has a higher response rate. After the results are in, the team sees that the online discount was more effective.

This is a great example of how you can use different tactics to influence your propensity scores. In this case, if a customer who receives a special email responds to the offer, then the next time the customer's risk score is calculated, it would go down (all other variables being held constant). Keep in mind that the customer might have other risk factors (as identified by the model) that move in the other direction. Regardless of the tactics that you employ, applying a test and control strategy is important. Without it, it's difficult if not impossible to determine (1) the effectiveness of your model in predicting the event, and (2) your ability to influence that event with a variety of tactics (which in and of themselves may have smaller, incremental objectives).

LAYERING IN COMPLEXITY

In a more complex scenario, you might want to test different messages within the at-risk population. You might even try different messaging for different risk deciles or other sub-segments. There are other considerations in defining the test-and-learn approach. If you're going to split out different segments of your population, you need to ensure that you have a statistically meaningful sample size.

Another consideration is complexity: Your ability to execute and monitor a wide variety of tactics. In one organization, its outbound campaigns included one of eight phone numbers that were used for marketing campaigns. The organization ran so many concurrent campaigns that the same phone numbers were being included on multiple campaigns. This meant that it didn't have the ability to tie any customer action back to a single campaign, and no way to know if its tactics were effective.

Another organization created a series of customer segments but found that its manual outbound campaign process didn't support more than one campaign at a time. Each subsequent campaign required significant recoding. The organization lacked the automation necessary to execute a targeted segmentation strategy.

Don't fall into the trap of not planning for what you want to optimize (i.e., what behavior you want to influence) and what will be impacted or influenced by the changes. Make sure that quantifiable objectives are defined. Experiments run without hypothesis testing might provide some interesting information, but without rigor in the testing process it will be difficult to influence your key metrics.

INCORPORATING TEST-AND-LEARN INTO YOUR MODEL DEPLOYMENT STRATEGY

Our predictive models help us determine the likelihood of an event occurring for certain segments of our population. But just because we know that an event is likely to occur doesn't mean we automatically know how to influence the outcome.

There are a couple of different approaches to segmentation. Many organizations perform segmentation or use propensity models on their populations prior to the test and then tailor their message based on the segment and likelihood to respond. Instead of providing a single experience to an entire population, they can create different experiences based on consumer profiles. Testing can be performed on the different segments.

Some organizations run experiments on entire populations and then perform segmentation posttest to see if there are any defining attributes for people that responded to a particular offer or message. Additional testing can be performed on any resulting segments that shake out.

Segmentation plays an important role in the journey from non-personalized to personalized user experience. Ultimately, many organizations are moving to real-time optimization—where the user experience is personalized at the point of contact based on the customer's history, their profile, and their current interaction.

One organization had a predefined set of campaigns that it would send to all of its customers. There was no differentiation in the messaging or channel. It created a number of predictive propensity models and teased out some really interesting segments in its customer population based on their likelihood to do something (buy more products, be more loyal, etc.). For example, people who are more likely to be more loyal are (1) over the age of 40, (2) female, and (3) live in an urban area. They also hate direct mail and love shopping on the Internet. You get the point.

In theory, now that the organization knows who's more likely to do something, it can target that population with more relevant messaging. Unfortunately, most organizations do not have the ability to create unique content for each segment, or they underestimate the amount of time needed to build out the creative component.

There are three main components to a campaign: the ability to segment your population, the message and medium, and channel or context. There's no point in creating segments if you can't align relevant messaging, media, and context. In addition to investments in analytics and technology needed to support segmentation, organizations must equally invest in the message and the medium.

Our example organization identified four distinct segments in one of its propensity models. To effectively target those segments, each would need different messaging across different channels. The complexity of its campaign strategy just quadrupled! This is a simple example, but you can imagine what happens as the organization creates more propensity models and segments.

Just because you can create tons of microsegments doesn't mean that you need to. In our example, the organization combined the propensity scores with the segments so that it could prioritize and identify where it could have the biggest impact. The short-term plan included a series of targeted messaging for two segments, with plans to expand to four in a phased approach. This gave it the time to develop and test new messaging as well as build out capabilities for managing multiple campaign workstreams.

If you're just starting to use segmentation strategies in your marketing programs, don't overwhelm yourself with complexity. As you identify the relevant segments in your business, look for high-impact opportunities, but remember that your creative messaging can make the difference (but you have to test it!).

CREATING A CULTURE OF EXPERIMENTATION

Even as companies increasingly move toward data-driven strategies in shaping their businesses, the shift away from gut-feel or instinct can be challenging. Recognizing passive and active resistance in your business community to test-driven approaches is critical in moving forward. It can be difficult to convince the higher-ups to try risky and radical approaches in product development, pricing, or communication strategies, but the beauty of testing is that it allows you to run an experiment to investigate whether the idea should be pursued further. This culture of experimentation enables curiosity and provides a forum for exploration and breakthrough discovery. Testing allows you to say: I know we should do this action because we validated that it's the right thing to do!

If you're doing a lot of Web or mobile design as part of your strategy, a culture of experimentation also facilitates organizational decision making by streamlining the decision process. Since tests can be statistically validated, there's no need to involve an army of "experts" in each decision-making process. For example, you'll free up a lot of time in not having to discuss what's the right banner for your site or the best message for your high-risk customer—you'll have your tests to tell you that.

This requires courage! While we encourage you to think big, ask a lot of little questions to get there. When too many things are tweaked at once, it can be difficult to tease out and interpret the results. Exploration and refinement are complementary techniques, most effectively used together (top down and bottom up). Explore big wins while testing smaller changes. The smaller changes can inform how you think about larger strategies.

Consider creating a test-and-learn backlog similar to your analytic story backlog. Use the backlog as a place to capture all the great tests that you'd like to perform on your results. A similar prioritization mechanism can be used to try out different ideas.

FAILING FAST AND FREQUENTLY

It's not that organizations aren't running tests—you're just not running enough. Not every experiment will have the outcome that you want or you can use. But failed experiments provide value: Knowing that a particular change negatively impacts the outcome in a test is far better than rolling out a change to an entire population. Failed tests also challenge us to change our assumptions, and results help identify why those assumptions might be incorrect. It also allows the organization to free up resources to work on the things that matter.

Large web-based companies literally run hundreds of tests on their sites per day to optimize different metrics. While you might not have the capability (or need) to run this many tests, if you're not scaling up your capabilities, you're missing out on opportunities to learn. Scaling should be done strategically: Hypotheses need to be prioritized based on the potential return on investment (ROI), and while it would be nice to test everything, organizations typically have constraints (resources, cost, time).

WHO OWNS TESTING?

While testing skills are naturally aligned to the analytic team, organizations with mature test-and-learn capabilities typically have dedicated business resources who can design a test. Ideas for tests can come from anywhere, but your tester is crucial in helping the organization define and create the test, coordinate the resources to create the creative or content, and analyze the results of the test.

The test-and-learn function can either be centralized or decentralized. In the centralized model, a single team performs testing on behalf of the larger organization. While this may work for smaller organizations (or organizations with smaller test-and-learn needs), as you grow your test-and-learn capabilities, you don't want your centralized team to become a bottleneck.

As organizations mature, a decentralized testing model allows for business autonomy and independence, where product managers or business owners may own responsibility for tests on their product or function. A centralized testing or analytic team may still own execution. As your experimentation capabilities increase, you will want to encourage more local ownership of testing to help anchor the approach in the culture. In a fully automated test-and-learn environment in digital channels, product managers/business owners may even execute their own tests.

Regardless of your organizational model, bring your stakeholder communities together frequently to share results and gather new ideas. You'll need to coordinate resources across marketing, product, pricing, and operational teams. Engaging these groups continually throughout test-and-learn cycles helps cement a culture of experimentation within the organization.

GETTING STARTED

Scrum can also be applied to test-and-learn. In an agile test-and-learn process, teams may define testing sprints, where a sprint goal is outlined for a specified period. The team brainstorms all of the possible tests aligned to that organizational goal and begins execution.

Building a testing platform in-house may only be appropriate for large organizations with dedicated software engineers (e.g., Amazon's testing platform is integrated with website, product catalog, and customer database). This is appropriate when specialized experiment design at scale is needed, as it requires tight coupling with operational systems.

Testing capabilities may also be developed as an extension to an analytics platform. You need the ability to collect, organize, examine, and analyze large volumes of data to understand and improve user experience. Automating the feedback mechanism is essential to scaling up your test-and-learn capabilities. If you can't analyze your results effectively, you won't be able to identify what tests are effective and where you should go next. The more efficient your data collection and lead generation processes are, the easier it will be to integrate into your testing strategy. Everyone needs to trust the data that come out of a test; otherwise, you'll be focused on validating data, not analyzing outcomes.

Remember that a culture of experimentation is just that: Culture. Beyond the necessary analytic skills, data and technology platforms don't overlook these critical organizational and cultural areas in your test-and-learn journey:

Stakeholder engagement is important. As you're developing your testing strategy, don't forget to identify and engage your internal stakeholders. Find experiments that will result in early wins and showcase capabilities before running more contentious tests that might scare off skittish stakeholders.

Don't be overly complicated. Complex tests requiring multisystem integration should be avoided until you've reached a level of maturity (and trust with your stakeholders) where that's appropriate. Use iterative approaches that pick winners and move them to the next test.

Ensure business ownership. Partner your developers and product owners together and brainstorm for testing ideas. Implement the tests and take business ownership of the results. Let product owners guide the process.

Question assumptions. Ron Kohavi, who runs the Analysis and Experimentation group at Microsoft, says, "Most people are overly confident that their idea will work, but most ideas fail to deliver" (Kohavi, 2013). Information trumps intuition. Always ask why something is being done, and it will force people to think about metrics and data.

Define critical success metrics. Before you start experimentation, be clear on what the objective of the test is and the metrics you will use to evaluate success. Identify the consumer behavior you're looking to influence and make sure that you don't have competing organizational goals (e.g., sales versus traffic).

Encourage competition. You don't want testing to be seen as just another step in a process that already "works." Create internal competitions to uncover the best testing results. One organization held a "Next Top Model" competition as a play on the television show. Different teams from around the company self-organized and created predictive models and test scenarios.

Evangelize results. Share test results with your stakeholder community on a regular basis. This will help communicate the good work that you're doing and assist with organizational buy-in.

Continually improve. Testing is not a finite activity. Don't be satisfied even after you've come up with what you believe to be your best design. Continuous testing should always lead to more questions, ideas, and opportunities for future exploration.

In one organization, the marketing group uses an iterative test-and-learn process in its marketing campaigns. As the campaigns are designed and executed, results are used to continually adjust the campaigns going forward. Marketing automation tools allow the marketing group to create multiple variants of a campaign, and data analysis drives a closed-loop measurement process. Creativity still remains an essential component of the marketing process, but data provide the connection between creativity and meaning.

SUMMARY

The process of experimentation through test-and-learn inevitably generates more questions than answers; each new question becomes an opportunity for additional experimentation. Not every test, however, will generate amazing (or even interesting) results. You may run many tests that fail. See failure as an opportunity to question assumptions and ask questions: It leads to new ideas and hypotheses.

CHAPTER 19

Operationalizing Your Model Deployment Strategy

At the beginning of our book, we discussed three types of analytics: informational, directional, and operational. Once the model development process and the business implementation planning are complete, a new iteration of work begins. In this section, we'll select our final model and prepare it for operational deployment. In some cases, our best model for deployment may not be the best model in terms of performance: For certain business problems, simpler may be better (see Figure 19.1).

FINDING THE RIGHT MODEL

Before we get to deployment, we need to determine which models will need to be put into production. In our modeling project, our data scientists used a number of different modeling techniques and created many different models. The models are fairly similar in terms of their ability to predict the target (likely to churn) as well as the predictive variables.

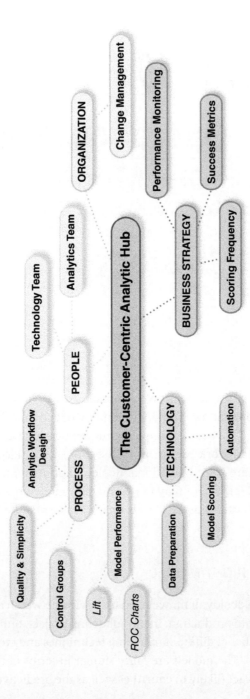

Figure 19.1 Operationalized Model Deployment Considerations

If you have many models performing similarly, you have some options for considering which ones will be deployed.

The primary metric used to select the best model is lift. Lift measures how effective a predictive model is by comparing the outcomes obtained both with and without the model. Let's take a look at a decile lift chart in Table 19.1 for a simple response model.

In this example, 120,000 leads were pulled from a historical customer table and scored with the model. The output shown in Table 19.1 is ranked high to low on its predictive score (probability of accepting an offer, also called conversion) and grouped by decile. We total the actual number of sales (remember, we're still looking at historical data) in each decile and divide by the number of leads in the decile to get the conversion score. The overall conversion score for the entire population (all 120,000 leads) is 0.9 percent. The lift in each group is calculated by dividing the conversion rate for each decile by the overall conversion rate (0.9%). Therefore, if you were to only contact leads in the first group, your conversion rate would be 2.8 percent, which is 3.3 times greater than if you chose a group at random from the overall population (with a 0.9 percent conversation rate). If you typically contact 30 percent of new leads, you would calculate the cumulative conversion rate at the third decile (617 out of 36,000), which is 1.7 percent and nearly double the average rate. If one was comparing potential

Table 19.1 Example Lift Chart

Decile	Number of Leads	Number of Sales	Conversion Rate	Lift
1	12,000	340	2.8%	3.3
2	12,000	152	1.3%	1.5
3	12,000	125	1.0%	1.2
4	12,000	104	0.9%	1.0
5	12,000	98	0.8%	0.9
6	12,000	67	0.6%	0.6
7	12,000	50	0.4%	0.5
8	12,000	38	0.3%	0.4
9	12,000	32	0.3%	0.3
10	12,000	18	0.2%	0.2
Total	120,000	1,024	0.9%	

models, you would compare the lift at specific deciles to determine which model would be most beneficial.

The model with the best lift may not be the best choice if the current environment has changed or is likely to change from the environment from which the model was developed. For example, if interest rates are found to be a predictive variable and they have been very low during the testing period, but rates are likely to rise in the near future, this attribute has not been adequately modeled using the historical data. Also, the model with the best lift might be overfitted, which means that it works best when the future environment is exactly the same as the past.

Another technique used to compare models is the receiver operating characteristic (or ROC) curve (see Figure 19.2). The curve graphically represents the lift chart, but can also be summarized with one number: the area under the curve.

The way to read this graph is that the red line represents the expected leads if no predictive model was used. In other words, we would expect a constant conversion rate regardless of the random sample of leads. So if we used 20 percent of the leads, we would capture 20 percent of the total sales, and if we used 60 percent of the leads, we would capture 60 percent of potential sales. The blue

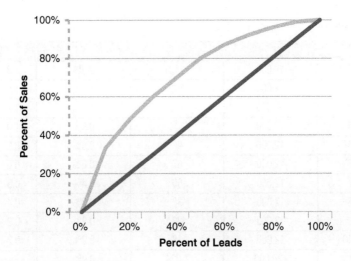

Figure 19.2 Example ROC Curve

indicates the lift we receive by using the model to select which leads to follow up on rather than using them all. If we use them all, we end up with the same number of sales. However, if we choose to use only the top 50 percent of the leads, we'll capture 80 percent of the sales (340 + 152 + 125 + 104 + 98)/1024 = 80 percent versus 50 percent if the selection was random. A perfect model is one in which we only snag the convertors, and that would be the curve represented by the green dashed line in the graph. Although that would be the Holy Grail of predictive modeling, it's not likely to ever happen.

The lift charts and ROC curves are just two examples that are widely used in model comparison and validation. Most predictive modeling tools will generate an additional series of model diagnostic scores that can be used as well. But having a great model is not the only consideration when determining which model to use.

Simplicity over Complexity

Let's say that the analytic team comes up with a great predictive model that has 30 variables in it. You have to analyze the organizational and technical costs of supplying those 30 variables on an ongoing basis. If you can build a really good model that performs almost as well and only has eight variables, then that might be a better model to put into production.

It is important to be judicious in the number of variables in your model. A model that has half the number of variables as another model but 10 percent less cumulative lift at a chosen decile can be superior after implementation for another simple reason: *less chance of imple-mentation errors.* Large, analytically mature organizations may not have these constraints, and in those cases model lift generally wins. Either way, an element of business judgment and keeping a keen eye on your technology capabilities are essential components of your model deployment strategy.

How Deep Do We Go?

If we go back to the previous decile table, we see that our model starts losing its predictive power after the third decile. What this means is that for 70 percent of our population, our model can't predict the outcome any better than random selection. Is this a bad model? Absolutely not—it just means that you'll want to limit your treatment option for the top 30 percent. Another business consideration in model deployment is deciding how deep to go into the deciles. For example, if 30 percent of your customer base contains three million customers, it might get a little expensive to engage with every person in that population. You wouldn't want to create some kind of treatment that directed all three million people to your call center at the same time. The two main considerations are: When does our model start to lose predictive power, and how many people can we engage with?

We can't say it enough: Don't forget to carve out a control group. Otherwise, you will have no way to gauge the effectiveness of your treatment strategies.

WHAT IS AN OPERATIONAL MODEL PROCESS?

Once the team has created a model that it wants to score on an ongoing basis, the model workflow (all of the data ETL work and model algorithm) needs to be turned into a repeatable process. Let's look at another example.

In Figure 19.3, we have an insurance claim intake process. Let's say you get into a car accident. One of the first things you'll do is call your insurance company to file a claim. The claims representative starts the claim process with you, takes down some information, and enters it into a claims management system (CMS). The data captured by the claims representative triggers a predictive model in the CMS, which is used to determine the likelihood that a claim is fraudulent. For that model to score the claim, it requires a certain set of data inputs. The output, or score, is then used to trigger different workflows within the claims process. If the fraud score was high, your claim might be routed to an investigator. If your score is low, the claim might be processed automatically. The underlying data and technology workflows supporting this process must be IT compliant.

The challenge that many organizations face is the transition from model development to deployment. Remember that our analytic process often takes a lot of disparate data sources and merges them

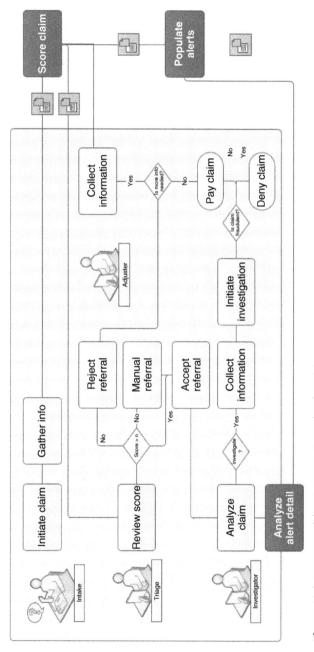

Figure 19.3 Insurance Claims Process—Operational Model

233

together in interesting and unique ways that boost the predictive lift of our model. These transformations aren't part of how the IT department typically captures and stores data. So when it comes time for deployment, the IT department struggles to figure out all of the post-processing work the analysts have done. It needs to be able to reproduce that work efficiently in a production environment.

GETTING YOUR DATA IN ORDER

Early on in our analytic projects, we're often not sure that the model development process will yield something meaningful. As a result, many teams don't prepare in advance. However, if we've done our job in the model development phase of our project using our agile analytic development process, our quality practices, and integrating our IT partners throughout the process, the transition from development to production doesn't have to be so painful.

Most commonly, the analytic team produces analytic results and then ends up managing the ongoing deployment process itself (this is a terrible use of analyst time!). Sometimes analytic teams create a deliverable and throw it over the wall: The business and IT can do with it what they want. Neither scenario is sustainable and has a serious impact. Here's an example: After the model development work is complete, the analytic team assumes that they're done. This results in two likely scenarios: Whatever has been developed is thrown over the wall to IT, and it becomes "their problem"; or the IT team disavows the deployment work and pushes it back onto the analytic team. In the first case, IT will spend a huge amount of time and resource effort to rebuild the model development process in a manner that's both automated and sustainable; in the second case, the analytic team ends up taking on technical production work that they're often ill-suited to manage.

In our agile analytic development methodology, both IT and/or dedicated data integration specialists play an active role throughout the model development process. Having that expertise available helps the analytic team to make better upfront data and technology decisions. Analytic teams typically suffer from several problems that contribute to increased model development and deployment cycle time. Here are some possible challenges:

- Development and execution of ETL and model scoring code on the desktop PCs are difficult.

- Code is poorly documented.

- Poorly written code leads to manual execution of coding steps and inefficient use of computing resources.

- Code is executed in the wrong environment. With the advent of in-database processing and other appliance and Hadoop-based data-management platforms, modelers need to understand where code is most effectively executed to take advantage of performance and scalability.

- Desktop-based code development and lack of technical standards reduces the extensibility of code (i.e., the code's ability to be reused).

The development of coding standards, as outlined in Chapter 15, "Building in Quality and Simplicity," can address many of these issues. If you analyze most "production" modeling code, you'll find that it often mirrors the thought process of the modeler, with data ETL, exploratory analysis, and quality checks interspersed throughout their workflow. This makes it difficult to identify and extract artifacts needed as part of the model documentation process. Beyond creating good technical and coding habits, a few other areas can also be addressed.

Automate Model-Ready Data Processes

Another practice that analytic teams can employ—especially if they're working with the same data sources over and over—is to create model-ready datasets. These are datasets that are prepared and loaded on a recurring basis. They are prestructured for modeling work, meaning that the information is aggregated to a one-row-per-customer (or whatever aggregation level you're modeling at) level. Teams that work continuously on the same business problem (credit card risk, insurance claims, marketing, etc.) generally find that they can build several model-ready datasets to cover the majority of their model development work (sandbox data environments can be made available for prototyping new data sources).

A primary benefit of standardizing the preparation of these ETL flows and model-ready datasets is that quality control checks can be built into the process. Data transformations can be standardized as well. Having this work done in advance means that modelers will spend less time on routine (and inconsistent) data preparation work and more time on analysis.

So Who Owns It?

In many organizations, the analytic team is performing the data extracts and creating model-ready data (and mini-data warehouses and datamarts). We recommend that these processes be moved to IT, where they can be more effectively supported and maintained.

> One analytic team managed a separate datamart that fed off of the corporate data warehouse. In general, the data quality from the warehouse was pretty good, but the team was still performing a number of clean-up routines on the data post-extraction. Since the data-quality work was performed outside of the data warehouse, none of the cleanup work was fed back to the warehouse. There was no formal mechanism for communicating changes in the source data to the analytic team, so the team continually had to profile and cleanse the same data sources. The volume of data coming in made this approach unsustainable: "We have so much data coming in, we can't have every modeler trying to figure out what's different."

In a typical process, an analytic team might pull from dozens of different internal and external data sources. If the teams are doing a lot of desktop PC work, each analyst may replicate the data extraction process. Streamlining and centralizing the data preparation process in advance can dramatically improve development, processing, and deployment cycle time.

What If I Can't Automate This Process Right Now?

If you can't automate the process in advance, don't worry. If you're working on a brand new project with lots of unknown data sources, then you obviously won't be able to do this up front. But as you go through your new model development process, consider the following:

Leverage your technical best practices. Down the road, if your model development process needs to be automated, your workflow will be cleaner and simpler to hand off to a different team member or technology group.

Considering hiring professional ETL developers on the analytic team. If that is not possible, have IT allocate one to you for important projects. In many large-scale analytic organizations, ETL development specialists are dedicated to the team. They don't participate in the model development process, but when data scientists believe that their model is ready for prime time, then the ETL resource streamlines the code and makes it production ready. If hiring a full-time developer doesn't make sense, then borrow someone in the organization with that skillset who can help.

Make sure ETL cleanup tasks are included in your product backlog. Good ETL is important. By making sure that production data stories are included on the product backlog, they are less likely to be forgotten or overlooked.

Remember: Don't automate or put bad processes into production. It will come back to haunt you.

DETERMINE MODEL SCORING FREQUENCY

Now that you have your data sorted out, the next step is to determine how frequently your model will need to be scored. On the surface, scoring is a really simple process. Scoring is the process of applying a predictive model algorithm to a set of data. The model development process determines which variables are important to the model algorithm. In production, those variables are isolated in a dataset, the algorithm is applied, and a score is generated.

How often do we need to score? There are a lot of factors that go into this decision. First, do you have a short-tail or a long-tail event that you're trying to predict? If your model predicts which movies somebody might like to watch, your recommendation engine needs to score that interaction in real time. Real-time scoring uses information gathered in real time and incorporates that with a predictive model to return a propensity score. Real-time scoring has been widely used by e-tailers, financial services, and insurance, and is making big headways into other consumer-focused industries.

Additional examples include the following:

Credit Card Decisions Have you ever applied for instant credit online? Real-time scoring engines use risk models and combine with other information about you gathered from external data sources. Based on the information provided (and verified), you may get an instant decision on credit along with a credit limit.

Purchase Recommendations Ever see the "people like you bought these items" on a website? Using your purchase history, current browsing information, and propensity models, retailers can provide more relevant offers.

Personalized coupons Based on purchases you make at the grocery store, for example, you might receive a coupon on your receipt for items that you are more likely to buy based on your purchases.

Not all real-time decisions are based on real-time information. The decision is made in real time using a combination of current information and precalculated scores (weekly, monthly, or whatever the right frequency is). Real-time decisioning is often coupled to business rule engines, where the score might be used as a decision point (i.e., propensity score greater than 50 percent, then do this, else do that ...).

Here's a more detailed example of a real-time offer with a batched score. The score is delivered in real time, but has been precalculated:

> Based on our customer profile, interaction history, and eligibility for specific products and their likelihood to respond to a given offer, we can determine what the optimal offer is for them through the use of analytically driven decisioning within the workflow. In this financial services example, the customer logs into the retirement page on the website to check the account balance. In real time, an engine behind the scenes determines a number of offers that the customer is eligible for. Based on the customer's propensity to respond to a particular offer, that

offer is presented to the customer on the website in real time. If our customer decides not to respond to that offer (e.g., raise the contribution rate), information about that interaction is stored and a follow-up email is sent a few days later. Static propensity scores are stored in a customer history file. These static scores may be generated on a monthly or weekly basis.

Our example business workflow provides a conceptual view of the customer logging into the website. Depending on what that customer does on the website, data from that interaction is captured and used to surface a recommendation to the customer in real time (see Figure 19.4).

For most models, cores are created and retrieved on a periodic basis or maybe even on an ad-hoc basis. If I'm an insurance company, for example, I might score my policyholders every six months, or whenever their policy period ends. Or I might generate scores on an as-needed basis for a marketing campaign that goes out on an infrequent basis.

It's also about the frequency of the data in your model. You need to look at the variables in your model and see how frequently those data sources are refreshed. If certain variables use data that's only updated once a month, you can either score on a monthly basis using the refreshed data, or score more frequently on stale data, and pick up the refreshed data when it is available.

One thing you will want to do is to create a plan for storing historical model scores. This will help determine the effectiveness of your model. When model scores start to drift, the model is losing its predictive power and should be reevaluated.

MODEL PERFORMANCE MONITORING

It's natural to want to know immediately how well a model is working but sometimes the data needs time to develop. This development period can be relatively short for a response model—send out an email or direct mail solicitation and it may be just days to a few weeks to capture 90 percent of the responses. Another example would be a recommendation engine: Someone either takes a recommendation or doesn't

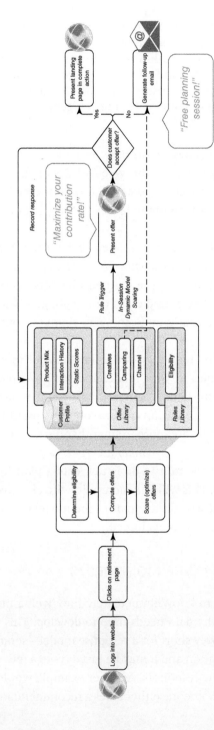

Figure 19.4 Designing a Conceptual Business Workflow

and the event happens immediately. In other scenarios (the insurance industry, for example) it may take a year, a typical policy period, to determine how well the model is working and if the company's overall loss ratio has decreased. Even when monitoring a long-tail event, there might be interim metrics that can be agreed upon to get an early read on the model's impact. These model performance metrics fall into our test-and-learn strategy: We're measuring our ability not only predict an event, but measure the effectiveness of our treatment strategy.

As noted, the model performance will deteriorate over time. The analytic team needs to put a performance monitoring strategy in place to evaluate the ongoing predictive power of the model. Here are some commonly used metrics to evaluate model performance:

Variable Profiles Remember that your model was built on a specific set of data at a specific point in time. The values within the variables can change (due to business factors, system changes, etc.) and the introduction (or reduction) of values will impact your model's performance.

Score Distribution Stability Over time, if you see the distribution of scores begin to drift, this is a good indication that the model should be reevaluated. Changing business conditions can dramatically impact the effectiveness of your model.

Overall Performance Lift Assessment Evaluation of predicted and target values for a model across time. This assessment monitors the lift given by the model at certain decile breakpoints.

The analytic team will need to determine thresholds for these metrics to determine when a business event should be remodeled.

ANALYTICS—THE SUCCESS TO PLAN FOR

The technical success of your implementation is an important aspect of your operational model deployment strategy. Equally important is preparing your business stakeholders and potentially customers that will be impacted by your new analytic process. The larger and more business-critical your project, the more important it becomes to have a change management strategy. After all, good analytics **should** change your business!

One organization was in the process of implementing an enterprise-level strategic analytic application—if they're successful, these analytics will not only be a game-changer for this organization but will drive enormous change in how they perform certain business processes. For this organization, the analytics weren't the problem, and getting the analytics embedded into the operational systems weren't the problem. The challenge was that the analytics significantly changed the standard operating procedures within their organization. In this instance, this organization found itself unprepared for managing that change, and as a result, stumbled with getting their internal business community (the people responsible for acting on the analytics) on board.

Think about it. How many organizations truly understand the implications of analytic initiatives on their organization? How many stakeholders cry success prematurely when the project is delivered according to its technical specifications? How do you ensure that your project will deliver the intended business results and achieve high user adoption? Change management: It's essential now, more than ever, as you're looking to analytics to drive organizationally strategic programs.

One health insurance benefits provider began to use analytics to improve the accuracy and consistency of their fraud detection process: *"Typically, the [investigative units] have provided training to adjusters on the [fraudulent] "flags" when they're in the field. We hope that adjusters recognize the flags and inform the investigators—but what we found was that most of the referrals into the investigators came from a tiny group of adjusters; they weren't consistently used. We're making it easier by providing the information that they need to make better decisions and referrals. We've started to implement predictive models and ... [we can use those models to] help educate the adjuster in following their instincts. We're finding that our mindset needs to change from going to a reactive to a proactive model."*

In this example, the team quickly recognized the change management needed to transform the organization. Enhanced fraud-detection techniques drove changes in how their field investigative units performed their jobs, how they interacted with information, and how their work was prioritized. In many cases, the team that performs the analytic work to support these initiatives is separate from the groups that have to work with output. Without the support of these end users, the initiative will be a failure.

> Another organization implemented a predictive segmentation model to target specific field sales reps at risk of attrition. After the model development, the business unit went through a training and education process. The first training session included the sales desk and the internal sales team. The presenters defined predictive modeling, identified the data used in the modeling process, and explained the outcome of the model: the probability or score a producer would receive based on the segmentation criteria. The explanation and education at this level were extremely important because some of the predictive scores were out of line with the organization's "gut feel," leading the sales team to doubt the model's validity. With the process well understood, the organization more readily adopted the campaign. Since the internal sales reps would be responsible for reaching out to these at-risk reps, buy-in was essential.

More often than not, there's a human that's making a decision based on your analytic output. Poorly implemented analytics pose a danger: Business users with a poor understanding of analytics can undermine the initiative by deviating from your analytic output. Organizations that recognize and address these challenges up front and work to educate business users will be most successful.

SUMMARY

We created a predictive model, and I bet you thought we were done! Not even close. Once we close out our model development work, we need to select the "best" model for the business, and that decision is not solely based on the model's predictive power. Once we have our model, we need to align our test-and-learn strategy to the model's ability to predict an event. Once we know which model to use and how the business will use it, we can develop our data strategy. A best practice is to prepare the modeling datasets in advance, but for new projects, using our technical best practices and the help of our IT partners will help smooth the transition process from development to production. Scoring frequency is dependent on how the scores will be used to influence your targets' behavior. The analytic team must develop a plan for monitoring the ongoing performance of the predictive model to determine its long-term effectiveness. While the technical implementation is important, keeping an eye on the changes happening within your people-centric processes is critical.

CHAPTER 20

Analytic Ever After

Still need a starting place? Feeling a little overwhelmed? If you know that your organizational engagement model and analytic delivery processes need to improve, but you don't know where to start, begin with an assessment of your current state capabilities across the analytic lifecycle. It can be helpful to validate the work you're currently doing today against the capabilities we've outlined in this book, but we recommend using it as a guideline. You'll want to add in other aspects that are unique to your analytic team and organization. A pilot project provides a good starting place for proving out your new deliver capabilities. Once you gain confidence and momentum, then you're ready to start scaling up.

BEGINNING YOUR JOURNEY

The first phase of your analytic process improvement initiative is to determine what needs to change within the process, who will be affected, who will be involved, how changes will impact the organization or your customers, and what techniques you can use to address different opportunities. Certainly, you can use agile methods to address problems across the ecosystem, but they might not always be appropriate. Before you go agile, determine how agile you really need to be. Also, keep in mind that the organizations that are most successful with agile are the ones that prepare for it. Consider Table 20.1.

As you start your analytic journey, ensure that your team has strong foundations for agility. For example, it will be difficult for the analytic team to use Scrum if the rest of the organization hasn't bought into the concept. If the analytic team doesn't have the infrastructure it needs, its ability to meet the sprint commitments will be compromised. If the organization doesn't support collaborative decision making, then the team will be challenged to define the work on its terms.

Most importantly, the organization needs agile leadership to succeed. Agile is transformational: You're moving away from a command-and-control decision-making structure toward a team-empowered approach. You're also deeply engaging your business and technology partners in the analytic process. You'll need to educate them on how analytics integrate into the business, and also how to work effectively together as the analytic development work progresses.

Your first step is to determine if agile is a good fit. If you've answered positively to the questions already outlined, or are working toward addressing them, then you're a good candidate for increasing agility. In fact, start an improvement backlog. Highlight areas that the organization and the team need to work on.

SUPPORTING THE ANALYTIC TEAM

The Agile Manifesto tells us to value *individuals and interactions over processes and tools.* When people are valued over processes, this positively impacts how teams are organized and motivated. Leaders within an agile organization uncover their people's needs and motivational factors, aligning them with the right tasks and responsibilities. Agile leaders create an environment that fosters collaboration and transparency, putting the needs of the team above their own to generate higher levels of productivity. Within the organization, there are several roles that agile leaders assume (coaches, managers, and leaders) and several attributes that define agile leadership.

Table 20.1 Questions to Ask When Deciding Whether to Be Analytically Agile

Capability	Questions to Ask
Strategic	• Think about the overall goals for your business: Does your analytic program respond to those needs? • Is there a sense of urgency behind the strategic goals? How does that translate into organizational priorities and success factors? • Is there a shared understanding of the strategic need across business functions/units?
Organizational	• How is the strategic direction communicated to teams? Does it facilitate the coordination of work activities? • Are there mechanisms in place for evaluating and improving business processes that span across the organization? If not, what are the mechanisms for coordinating across teams? • Does the current organizational structure impede or facilitate the coordination of analytic work? • Are incentive models across teams aligned?
Cultural	• Is information shared freely throughout the organization? If not, what/where/who are the bottlenecks? • Does the organization empower or impede teams from the decision-making process?
People	• How is the organization keeping up with analytic competency development? • Do analytic resources have meaningful job experiences and career paths?
Processes	• Does the analytic team currently have a standard process for working on analytic projects? • Are the processes clearly defined and well understood? • Are the processes integrated across teams? • What works well and what needs to be improved?
Technology	• Does the analytic team have access to the necessary tools and technologies to do its work? • Is it supported outside of the analytic organization?
Data	• Does the existing data infrastructure support analytic needs? • Is the data well understood?

A common management complaint about agile methodologies is the feeling of a loss of control over their resources and the project process. Functional managers still hold an important role for agile teams by empowering teams through delegating responsibility. While the managers don't relinquish all control, they can define an authority level for the team and trust that the team will carry out those responsibilities. Managers also help the team create trust.

Agile leaders embrace agile values and principles alongside their teams. It's not uncommon in many organizations for managers to not "get" agile, especially in organizations that are transitioning from waterfall project methodologies (or no project methodology!) to agile. Embedding agile into an organization's culture requires management support and understanding. Agile managers "see the whole" and make decisions based on the greater good of the organization (as opposed to making localized decisions).

While the ScrumMaster can assist with removing organizational impediments, the leader is key to the process. The leader helps bring different internal groups together and remove unnecessary communication boundaries between both internal and external teams.

THE IMPORTANCE OF AGILE ANALYTIC LEADERSHIP

Lyssa Adkins (2010) tells us, *"Agile is far more than an alternate project management methodology. It's great for that, but that is also the weakest expression of it."* What she means is that agile taps into our personal sense of purpose and standards for excellence when it's well executed. Agile leaders facilitate the process by guiding the team to agile excellence.

Agile frameworks, Scrum in particular, are deceptively simple. Agile leaders provide the team with a continuing set of values, practices, and principles to adhere to. The agile leader wears many different hats in the process. In addition to the functions listed in the figure below, they help the teams search for the next breakthrough idea in their processes. Good agile leaders model behavior for their teams.

Agile leaders are active participants in ensuring the team has the appropriate organizational environment for success. While they retain many traditional management functions, they delegate certain levels of authority to the team. Agile leaders practice both servant and adaptive leadership, working on behalf of the team, and promote an agile culture to generate and sustain awareness of agile practices. Agile leadership traits for self-mastery apply to all team members: They are emotionally aware, practice active listening, and work to resolve conflicts through negotiation. Agile coaches can help the team on the path to agile excellence by promoting agile values, practices, and principles.

FINDING A PILOT PROJECT

A good way to find out if using agile approaches in your analytic delivery cycles is suitable is to select a pilot project. An ideal pilot is one that is meaningful enough to show value to the organization, but manageable enough so the team doesn't get overwhelmed. The project should be of importance since you want to gain the organization's attention. Also consider the duration: Ideally, select something that can be completed start-to-finish in two to four months. Start with a collocated team, as it will make communication and collaboration easier. When you get more comfortable with agile, then consider scaling out to distributed teams. The pilot project needs to include business and technology support and stakeholders in addition to the analytic team; but find the right people. Your pilot team needs people who want to innovate.

Once you have a pilot project lined up, identify success criteria for the agile process. What do you want the results of this agility pilot to prove out? Faster delivery, better quality of results, improved engagement or collaboration? Once you have established the goals for the pilot, then you can begin to ramp up your pilot team.

SCALING UP

While agile works best with co-located teams, organizations with multisite and offshore development models can scale agile with some careful considerations. Even in a multisite environment, Scrum practices still apply, but the team has to work a lot harder to achieve the same collaboration benefits that a colocated team will experience.

In multisite development, the size of the overall team does not grow, but instead work is distributed across different parts of the organization. If possible, keep the number of sites to a minimum. Even short distances between team members contribute to communication problems.

Agile coaches can help accelerate capabilities by providing teams with guidance, expertise, and objective feedback. As teams begin to scale, there are a variety of organizational structures that can be utilized. Coordination across partners and geographic distribution creates a new challenge for the agile team. Communication and collaboration remain paramount for successful agile delivery.

As organizations scale up their development practices, the need for agile leadership becomes more important. If you're working with an offshore partner, make sure that the on- and offshore teams have a consistent set of agile values and principles. In fact, it might be the partner that is encouraging an agile approach. Feedback loops between the two teams are essential. One way to get this started is to hold a kickoff agile workshop to educate both parties in agile analytic values:

Share the core values behind your agile analytic framework. Don't focus on the nuts and bolts of Scrum, but discuss the values within The Agile Manifesto and how they apply to your organization.

Introduce your team's agile processes to the group. Define terms that will be used: product backlog, sprint planning and execution, reviews, retrospectives, releases, and so on.

Clarify roles and responsibilities. Highlight how your agile analytic process is different from the status quo.

Walk through a mock sprint. As part of your workshop, set up a mock analytic sprint and show the group how the process works.

While tele-presence and communication technologies help bridge the distance between multisite teams, they are not a panacea. Time-zone differentials exacerbate the problem as teams lose the ability to communicate and collaborate in real time. Team dispersion will have a higher negative impact when (1) there are significant cultural and language differences; (2) the team has never met in person, resulting in low trust; and (3) the team members only communicate asynchronously (i.e., through email).

Distributed teams need to define a common language with a shared vocabulary. This can include the language of the business or the analytic project, or specific process training on Scrum/agile methods. Making team members go through a common training class or program before joining the team will help ensure that team members have the same baseline knowledge. Agile coaches can also facilitate this process. Establishing common technical practices and a consistent multisite "definition of done" are key as well.

Avoid an "us versus them" mentality by creating liaison roles to bridge the different team development sites or organizations, and reduce communication bottlenecks by not enforcing a "single point of contact" structure between teams. Detailed requirements, prototyping, and acceptance of test-driven development can decrease ambiguity. Be cognizant of communication and collaboration barriers. Leverage collaboration technologies such as wikis to support interaction where appropriate.

THE END OF THE BEGINNING

At the end of the day, if you can take just *some* of the techniques and methods that we've outlined in this book and use them to improve your ability to deliver quality analytic results regardless of organizational constraints, then that's a success. It's okay to be agile enough. Your goal isn't to implement out-of-the-box Scrum: Your focus should be on increasing business agility—getting high-quality deliverables out to market sooner. You're not agile just because you use Scrum. Also remember that agility is a continuous journey: There's always more to improve on. Go forth and champion change!

Sources

Adkins, L. (2010). *Coaching Agile Teams*. Boston, MA: Pearson Education, Inc.

Beck, K., Beedle, M., Bennekum, A., Cockburn, A., Cunningham, W. et al. (2001). "The Agile Manifesto." Retrieved July 1, 2013 from: agilemanifesto.org

Cockburn, A. (2008). "Information Radiator." Retrieved online at http://alistair.cockburn.us/Information+radiator

Cohn, M. (2004). "User Stories Applied for Agile Software Development." Boston, MA: Pearson Education, Inc.

Fowler, M. (2009). "Technical Debt Quadrant." Retrieved online from: http://martinfowler.com/bliki/TechnicalDebtQuadrant.html.

Kohavi, R. (2013, December 12). "Online Controlled Experiments: Introduction, Insights, Scaling, and Humbling Statistics." Retrieved from: http://www.infoq.com/presentations/controlled-experiments

Leffingwell, D. (2007). *Scaling Software Agility: Best Practices for Large Enterprises*. Upper Saddle River, NJ: Addison-Wesley

Patton, J. (2008). "The New User Story Backlog Is a Map." Retrieved from: http://www.agileproductdesign.com/blog/the_new_backlog.html.

Pichler, R. (2010). *Agile Product Management with Scrum: Creating Products that Customers Love*. Upper Saddle River, NJ: Addison-Wesley.

Rubin, K. (2013). *Essential Scrum: A Practical Guide to the Most Popular Agile Process*. Upper Saddle River, NJ: Addison-Wesley.

Schwaber, K. (2009). *Agile Project Management with Scrum*. Redmond, WA: Microsoft Press.

Shore, J. & Warden, S. (2008). *The Art of Agile Development*. Sebastopol, CA: O'Reilly Media.

Takeuchi, H., and Nonaka, I. (1986, January). "The New New Product Development Game." *Harvard Business Review*. Retrieved online from: http://hbr.org/product/new-new-product-development-game/an/86116-PDF-ENG.

VersionOne (2013). "The 7th Annual State of Agile Development Survey." Retrieved from: http://www.versionone.com/pdf/7th-Annual-State-of-Agile-Development-Survey.pdf.

Wake, Bill (August 17, 2003). "INVEST in Good Stories and SMART Tasks." Retrieved from http://xp123.com/articles/invest-in-good-stories-and-smart-tasks/.

Index

Page numbers followed by *f* and *t* refer to figures and tables, respectively.